BEGGAR ON HORSEBACK

Beggar on Horseback

THE AUTOBIOGRAPHY OF
THOMAS D. CABOT

DAVID R. GODINE

BOSTON

Frontispiece: Chairman and President of Cabot Corporation (sketch by Harold Brett)

First published in 1979 by David R. Godine, Publisher
306 Dartmouth Street, Boston, Massachusetts 02116

ISBN: 0–87923-268-4   LCC: 78–70524

Printed in the United States of America

*Set a beggar on horseback
and he will ride a gallop.*

ROBERT BURTON
Anatomy of Melancholy

CONTENTS

	Foreword	ix
	Acknowledgments	xii
	Genealogy	xiii
I	Father and I	1
II	Flying and the War	9
III	Courtship and Marriage	17
IV	Mountaineering and the Family	23
V	Cabot and Carbon Black	44
VI	Diversification	70
VII	United Fruit Company	78
VIII	Government Service	83
IX	The Canoe	93
X	Sailing under the Jolly Roger	98
XI	Storms and Shipwrecks	109
XII	Skiing	122
XIII	First Aid	131
XIV	Hunting and Ranching	134
XV	Love of Unspoiled Islands	145
XVI	Travels	161
XVII	Higher Education	168
XVIII	Philanthropy	176
	Appendix	185

Foreword

SKI SLOPES—indeed, mountains of any kind—are good for getting at the truth of things. They quickly let you know who you are and can tell you something about your companions as well. That is why mountains are good places for making long-lasting friendships.

I first met Tom Cabot on the slopes of Aspen some 20 years ago, and we have skied there together every year since. He is a man who loves mountains, and has climbed, skied, and even mapped them in many parts of the world.

But mountains alone have never been nearly enough for him. You would have to add islands and sailing (he owns several islands off the coast of Maine); rivers and canoeing (half the metal canoes sold today incorporate his own personal design); skies and flying (he taught Army cadets how to fly Curtiss Jennies in World War I); woods and backpacking (he and his companions pioneered the route from Canada's Lake Louise to Jasper over the Continental Divide); fields and hunting (he has ridden to the hounds virtually everywhere from New England to Normandy); and the Caribbean and hidden treasure (he surely must be the only man in history to have organized a voyage under the Jolly Roger with three lawyers aboard drawing up papers for a charitable foundation to give away the loot).

For a Proper Bostonian who at sixteen spent a year in Arizona wrangling horses—only three years after that untamed territory had become a state—it is not surprising that unconventional globe-girdling was to become in later life a serious interest.

Even cataloging his travels becomes a fascinating exercise in elliptical references. Take the matter of islands. What are we to say of a man who can lightly toss off the sentence: "We especially enjoyed such less well known islands as Tierra del Fuego, Iceland, Greenland, Newfoundland, the Hebrides, Tahiti, Moorea, Bora Bora, Viti Levu, New Zealand, Madeira, the Azores, the Canaries, the Balearics, the Ionians, the Cyclades, the Dodecanese, Rhodes, Crete, Sicily, Malta, Gozo, Sardinia, and Corsica, as well as all the principal islands of the Greater and Lesser Antilles, some of the East Indies, the Galapagos, and several Alaskan islands."

Add these to "some horseback riding in Hungary"; "some bird watching on the tributaries of the Amazon"; and "two trips to Patagonia" and one would begin to think that Tom Cabot had given up on Boston. But no. Headquartered there, he built a modest family business into the world's leading producer of carbon black while pioneering much of the industry's technology.

He was elected an overseer of Harvard not merely once, but for an almost unprecedented second term, and quickly earned the title he probably cherishes most: "the biggest beggar in Boston." Having raised millions of dollars for Harvard and the other universities of the greater Boston area, he took on—at age seventy-one—a major consolidation of the Harvard Medical School's health care throughout the city, merging four hospitals into one corporate ownership, and building the new Affiliated Hospital Center.

Nor has he been content simply with the construction of facilities. He has been active in designing entire health maintenance organizations that effectively lower medical costs to consumers through preventive care, and through modifications of the immensely expensive adversary process in malpractice insurance programs.

As he notes characteristically: "An engineer thinks in terms of mechanical advantage or levers by which a small initial force can overcome large resistance. An industrialist thinks in terms of incentives by which he can get maximum productivity from his co-workers. I try to devise plans for approaching social problems by similar means."

It has been this dedication to the larger public interest that has prompted him to find time in an incredibly active and busy career for special tasks that needed attention in local, state, and federal government: everything from organizing a new water supply for Weston, Massachusetts, to promoting bipartisanship in foreign affairs by becoming a Republican Director of International Security Affairs in the Democratic Administration of President Truman.

Philanthropist, industrialist, civil servant, horseman, conservationist, engineer, sailor, explorer, fund raiser, mountaineer, pilot, skier, author: is there any limit to the interest and activities of Tom Cabot? If there is, I haven't uncovered it in twenty years of friendship.

The satisfying truth is that readers will find this volume precisely what an autobiography ought to be: a candid image of its author. Here he is, brimming with adventure, full of zest for life, devoted to goals beyond self, lean and tough in judgment, frugal and wise in advice.

"A life without dedication," he concludes, "can never be a happy one."

Agreed. And it's just not possible to imagine an undedicated —or an unhappy—Tom Cabot.

ROBERT S. McNAMARA

ACKNOWLEDGMENTS

I owe great thanks to the many friends who have given encouragement and comments, and especially to Ted Weeks for his invaluable advice and to David Godine for his skillful assistance.

Some who have participated in our adventures may feel disappointed that their presence was overlooked. If so, I hope they will allow me to apologize in person, for I would enjoy a swap of reminiscences.

Godfrey L. Cabot m. Maria Moors   Louis B. Wellington m. Louise Lawton

Thomas D. Cabot m. Virginia Wellington

Louis W.	Thomas D. Jr.	Robert M.	Linda	Edmund B.
m. Mary Louise Bass	m. Anne Flint	m. Charlotte Fitzpatrick	m. David G. Black	m. Mary D. Goodwin
James B.	Thomas D., III	Kathleen L. (Fitzgerald)	Sophia	Christina
Anne L. (Stewart)	Moors (Meyers)	Sara (Arshad)	Sandor	Virginia W., II
Godfrey L., II	Cecily (Klingman)	m. Maria Anagnostopulu	Jeremy	
Amanda (Connolly)	m. Mary McCarthy	Alexis		
Helen	Robert M.			
	Laura			
	James W.			

CHAPTER I

❦

Father and I

I CAN look back with satisfaction at my pioneering in the carbon black industry and in such outdoor sports as skiing and canoeing. To venture into new fields is exciting, and I would like to recall in these pages some of that excitement.

My Puritan ancestors came to build their lives in the hard land of New England. They may have come for reasons of religious intolerance or bigotry, but I am glad they sought freedom and adventure here where there are such opportunities for communion with nature and for a varied and challenging life.

Mine was not an altogether happy childhood. Ours was a competitive household. We were constantly reminded of duty—duty to God, to country, to family, and to oneself. Duty always overshadowed fun. We were governed by an ascetic father who lived by puritanical tenets. Hard work, self-denial, and self-improvement were his paramount concerns. Art, literature, and nature were to be studied rather than enjoyed. As a child, I was dominated by paternal orders. For the smallest disobedience I was taken into the library to lower my britches for a painful spanking. As an adolescent, avoiding sex, gambling, alcohol, tobacco, and even coffee is not in itself much of a hardship, but it does set one apart and make it difficult to develop friendships.

Father was a founder of the Watch and Ward Society and strong supporter of the Anti-Saloon League. The Watch and Ward tried to protect the public from all forms of vice: prostitution, pornography, gambling, and the misuse of drugs. From this effort he learned that the Boston vice ring and its lawyer had bought protection by bribing the District Attorneys of Suffolk and Middlesex Counties. In achieving his ambition to jail the proponents of Boston vice, he made it dangerous for any child of his to stray from the straight and narrow path lest it fall into a snare set by these masters of corruption. I never defied Prohibition, nor indeed had a drink of hard liquor until I was past thirty.

With Father there was no middle ground between good and bad. He collected facts rather than friends. Mother strove to follow his precepts but had despite herself a compassionate nature that gave her more understanding of people and of their shades of character. Social contacts were largely intellectual; famous scholars came to our house to converse on the latest discoveries in the world of science.

Neither parent had any interest or experience in woodcraft or camping. We never even went on picnics. We exercised for health, not enjoyment. We walked but never hiked, rowed but never sailed, played chess or word games but never games of chance or opportunity.

We lived in Cambridge almost in the shadow of Harvard. I was born there in 1897, the third of five children. Our home was then on Brewster Street in a four-family house, but we soon moved to 16 Highland Street where a frame house was built for us at a cost of $10,000. Nearby there were still many vacant lots where we could play. Although our Cabot ancestors had been rich and our Moors grandparents lived in a brownstone house in Back Bay and moved to a large manor house on the seashore at Cohasset for the summer, we lived very frugally. As children, we were taught to save every penny and wore handed-down clothes. To be sure, we had servants, usually Swedish immigrants, but we had no telephone until I was ten, and no electric lights or automobile until I was fifteen. We walked or bicycled to school and used the new electric trolley cars when we went to town. The horse cars I can dimly remember. For trips to other suburbs, we hired a cab from the livery stable. Although some of our more prosperous neighbors had their own horses and stables, with us walking was a duty, and I never saw either parent drive or ride a horse.

In winter our house was never really warm. Our furnace and cookstove were stoked with anthracite. Each day ice came by cart, groceries by wagon or pung, milk by gig, newspaper by a boy on a bicycle, and a lamplighter came afoot to light the gas lamps along the street. Suburban streets were gravel and only the main highways were of macadam. In those days this meant crushed rock bound with clay. Roads were narrow and shaded by trees. No modern freeways or even tar-bound roads existed until the automobile era.

Despite their austerity, our parents did encourage an interest in science. I built a wireless set when only eleven that had a hand-wound tuning coil, improvised condenser and coherer of iron filings as used by Marconi—but it wouldn't work. The coherer was soon replaced by a crystal detector and earphones given me by an aunt, and with this I could hear signals from the Crufts Laboratory nearby. Later I helped my brother Jim build a glider of laminated spruce, its frame covered with doped muslin. Probably we were fortunate that the first time we tried to fly it a wing strut broke, and it crashed before we got it off the ground. Jim was five years older than I, and given the severity of our family life, we were more competitive than affectionate.

Even more lethal were the chemical experiments in our attic. I wonder that we weren't asphyxiated making poison gases without a hood or proper ventilation. In these activities I was joined by my schoolmates Bill Castle, who later became a great medical teacher and researcher, and Delano Potter, who became a captain of sailing ships. We were too young to know the dangers but, wanting to impress our young friends, we demonstrated

the electric arc, the making of gunpowder, the destructive powers of strong acids and alkalies, and the production of such awful
gases as green chlorine and red nitric oxide. These may have
enhanced my interest in science, but I think it started with my
father who had studied chemistry at Harvard and in Europe before starting in the carbon black business which he built in the
gas fields of Pennsylvania and West Virginia.

Most of Harvard's famous professors lived in our neighborhood. I met many and came to know a few as neighbors rather
than scholars. William Pickering, the astronomer, lived next
door and walked each morning to Observatory Hill. I would
watch for his departure to walk with him toward my school on
Buckingham Street, not to enjoy conversation but to avoid at-
tacks from Irish boys bound for the parochial school on the hill.
As a lad of five or six, I lived in terror of these "Micks" who
were quick to pick a fight and much handier with their fists than
I. When unaccompanied, I would sneak through back yards, lie
in a privet hedge to see there were no bullies in sight before
crossing Sparks Street, then rush for a hole in the back fence of
our school.

Lawrence Henderson, a founder of bio-chemistry, lived in
our block and was a special friend because he taught me to
canoe. Percy Bridgman, the Nobel physicist, and a friend of
Father's, invited me to see his high pressure apparatus where I
had a chance to touch ice too *hot* to handle. T. W. Richards,
who won the Nobel Prize in chemistry, had a daughter, Patty,
who was my schoolmate and later married my friend Jim
Conant. It was Jim who introduced me to organic chemistry
before he became President of Harvard. R. DeC. Ward, the
climatologist, as he passed our house would be asked for a
weather forecast. Albert Sauveur, who later introduced me to
metallurgy, had a yard in which we often played, not because
of the yard but because of his lovely daughter Hortense, who
was my schoolmate.

A modern photograph of our old home at 16 Highland Street, Cambridge, built in 1898 at a cost of $10,000.

Father—Godfrey Lowell Cabot, about 1922.

Exploring the orchard
—aged three.

Making the school bully say "Sorry." Evans School, 1914, Mesa, Arizona.

Cliff dwelling in Superstition Mountains discovered by Major Brady, which stimulated our desire to explore Fish Creek.

Wading down Fish Creek to Salt River, 1914.

Virginia Wellington, sweet sixteen.

Working on Father's seaplane, designed by Starling Burgess, at its hangar on Misery Island off the beach at Beverly Farms, summer of 1915.

Plane in which I was to have made my first solo flight if it hadn't crashed earlier that morning.

Lieutenant Cabot, flying instructor, with cadet student and Curtiss "Jennie" plane.

A seasoned aviator with 2,000 hours of flying as instructor and pilot, and experience in nearly all types of planes used by the United States Army and Navy in World War I.

Virginia Wellington, a 1917 Boston debutante.

Courting at Gateways in the
summer of 1919.

Swimming at Cape Cod during the summer of 1919 before our engagement.

The house Father bought for us on the outskirts of Spencer, West Virginia.

For testing and repairing gas meters, I needed to carry a hundred pounds of tools, gauges, and spare parts.

Wedding party at Gateways, May 15, 1920. Left to right: Lydia Hall, Jim Cabot, Susan Baker, Henry Hall, Kitty Billings, Ralph Bradley, Linda Wellington, Jack Cabot, V.W.C., T.D.C., Alec Bright, Polly de Camp, Ned Billings, Margaret Ranney, Dudley Ranney, Jerome Johnson, Eleanor Bremer.

Father and I

Not all the professors in our neighborhood were scientists. I went to school with the children of F. Bocher (mathematics), A. B. Hart (history), G. L. Kittredge (English), G. P. Baker (drama), among others, and would sometimes meet their parents when playing at their homes in the afternoon. Bliss Perry and Le Baron Briggs would occasionally play scrub baseball with us in a vacant lot, and Lewis Johnson would ask us to tea to talk to our young malleable minds about the importance of civil liberties and women's suffrage.

Neighbor and neighborhood were really meaningful in those days before the automobile. Sidewalks and yards were where we greeted friends and doffed hats to ladies. Homes were for congeniality; afternoon tea was an occasion for guests. Books had not been displaced by television, nor conversation by the rush to new destinations.

Stimulated by my parents and by my teachers at Brown & Nichols School, I had passed all my exams for Harvard when barely sixteen and not yet mature enough for college life. Luckily my immaturity was recognized, and I was sent to Arizona to "grow up." Although I had learned a little about camping and woodcraft on my own in the woods of Belmont and Winchester, it was my year in the deserts and mountains of Arizona that really taught me to camp and fend for myself.

There, in the clear air and brilliant sun of southern Arizona, I developed a real love of the out-of-doors. How well I remember the purple hills of early dawn turning to orange with the rising sun. The smell of fresh dung in a corral and the plainsong of milling cattle in the dust still bring back pleasant memories. And the aptitude I developed for tracking, wrangling, packing, and guiding in those western mountains was to last a lifetime.

It was 1914 and Arizona had been a state for only three years. Theodore Roosevelt had tamed the floods of the Salt River, but not yet tamed the desert with irrigation. The rains were filling the lake at Roosevelt Dam sixty miles upriver from the school at Mesa and canals were being dug to bring under cultivation the arid land abutting our village and campus. There, at the Evans School, we lived each in our own cabin. Behind the cabins were a back-house and the horse corrals; in front was the main building where we ate, attended classes, and occasionally bathed. The cowboys still came to town with holsters and six-shooters, but Mesa was a village of law-abiding Mormons with few of the flamboyant vices of the traditional West. Phoenix, the capital, was a long ride by horseback usually attempted only by those schoolmates who wanted forbidden beer. The roads were dusty or muddy and there was one prototypical hotel with a wooden rail in front where we hitched our horses. Nowadays, a sprawling city has engulfed Phoenix and Mesa and much of that wild country, where greasewood, mesquite, and cactus of all sorts once grew.

My interest in exploration had come from reading in our home library the voluminous accounts of polar explorations by Nansen, Peary, Scott, Shackleton, Mawson and Stefansson. In Arizona, I now had the chance to do some real exploring. Although I was nominally in school, Mr. Evans, the headmaster who was known as "Prof," felt no necessity for advancing my formal education. He let me spend most of my time wandering in the desert or helping ranchers in the mountains with their cattle. This did far more for my future happiness than the reading of Latin and English literature. Under the guidance of Major L. F. Brady, one of the teachers and an ardent amateur archaeologist, I was taken on several trips into desert canyons looking for the cliff dwellings of pre-Columbian Indians. We explored the Superstition and Mazatzal Mountains and near the head of Fish Creek, we were thrilled to find ruins not previously reported. Brady was a little man, in his forties, very spry, and eager for us to descend the canyon all the way to the Salt River.

Father and I

We waded through narrow gorges which probably had never been visited before. I hate to think what would have happened had there been a cloudburst in the mountains. They won't be waded again, for the Horse Mesa Dam has now flooded the whole canyon. That was the first of my pioneering trips and led to others which I shall describe.

It was Major Brady from whom I bought my horse, a buckskin Indian pony, a real mustang born of a feral mare and trained by the Indians. He cost me $60, and when I left school, Brady bought him back for $50. The Major also taught me to pack a horse with either the one-man or the two-man diamond hitch.

The most important gain from this year in the West was my introduction to horses, for in time this led to my happy marriage to a girl who had been brought up with them. We first met at Mr. Foster's Dancing School, held on Friday afternoons in the ballroom of the Hotel Somerset, and attended, traditionally, by sub-debutantes. Virginia, then fifteen, was a junior at Miss Winsor's School. I was eighteen and a freshman at Harvard. Being short-sighted she wore horn-rimmed spectacles with thick lenses, but she had gorgeous blond hair, a peaches-and-cream complexion, an attractive smile, and she danced like a dream. As a Boston Cabot I felt a bit put down that even after the fourth time I had asked her for a dance she couldn't remember my name. Perhaps this was shyness; she must have heard, as Dorothy Parker later put it, that "Men don't make passes at girls who wear glasses."

In the spring my classmates Alec Bright and Ned Billings and I began to call on the Wellington sisters, Virginia and Linda, at their summer home, the "Gateways Farm" of Weston, where their family had a stable of riding horses. In June, Virginia came to a house party that my mother arranged at our summer place in Beverly Farms with the three of us and also our Cambridge neighbors, Betsy Bright and Dolly Thompson.

And when I went off to Plattsburgh that summer for military training, letters began to fly back and forth. By fall I must have been in love. I thought more about her than I did about my classes at Harvard—where I was proving to be a less than mediocre student. We often rode together on the Wellington horses and danced at debutante parties. We were both shy and unworldly youngsters who talked more about simple country pleasures than about the sophistication of the city, but our common interest in horses did more than anything to draw us together. Of course, we were much too young to talk about marriage, and even the chance that the war in Europe might engulf us was hardly mentioned.

Virginia had been brought up in a large, affectionate household. Louis Wellington, her father, had married Louise Lawton of New Bedford, and for the first seven years they lived at the old Wellington farm in Medford where their three daughters were born, Virginia being the middle one. Then Louis's older brother Arthur married his sister-in-law, Evelyn Lawton, and the two couples shortly agreed to dwell together: in winter in the lovely old house on Beacon Hill which had been built by Bulfinch a century earlier, and during the summer months at Gateways Farm with its ancient farmhouse, white picket fence, and red barns. It was a singularly happy arrangement. Virginia and her younger sister Linda were a devoted pair and together they brought up their much younger and very attractive double-cousin Nancy, who was later to marry Nicholas Danforth.

CHAPTER II

❧

Flying and the War

WHEN war broke out in Europe in 1914, Father predicted that we would inevitably be drawn into it. He had been interested in flight from boyhood and in 1903, when the Wrights flew at Kitty Hawk, Father wrote offering to finance their development. At the same time he wrote to his friends President Theodore Roosevelt and Senator Henry Cabot Lodge, Sr. to say that the "aeroplane" would be of great military and commercial importance, and that the government should not hesitate to negotiate for the patents.

Father was so disgusted with Wilson's pacifism that in 1914 he ordered an aeroplane designed by Starling Burgess to be built in Marblehead with a Sturtevant engine. It was a biplane with an extreme sweepback and no tail. It had only two ailerons for control, each activated by a separate stick beside the pilot. I took lessons in flying it which proved to be of very little help in flying anything else.

In April 1917, Father, who had been commissioned for active service as a Naval Aviator, offered to pay my tuition at the Curtiss Flying School near Buffalo, where my brother Jim was already enrolled. I took early exams and then left Harvard on what seemed to be my route to war. The Wellington sisters promised to wave as my train sped past Gateways Farm. So I prepared a billet-doux and threw it from the door of the Pullman; the note was recovered but, alas, was later lost. I think I may have been so bold as to sign it "C. Y. K.," but it was addressed to *both* sisters.

[9]

In Buffalo, Jim and I roomed in a boarding house in the city, which was ten miles from the flying field. So we bought motorcycles; Jim, who had been working and earning money, paid $300 for a new machine, but as I had to be more frugal, I paid only $30 for a very old model. When not actually flying, I spent hours tinkering with it and made it go so well that I beat Jim and several others in an informal race. I'm certain our motorcycle rides were more dangerous than our flying lessons.

My instructor was a nervous Englishman named Spratt. It was said that he had been let out of the RAF because of "shell shock." His nervousness encouraged my own fears when I flew with him, and I didn't think I had learned much when he announced I was ready to solo. My first flight alone was terrifying, made the more so because it took place shortly after I had had my first contact with sudden death. I had been behind the hangar in the back-house with my pants down when a low-flying plane crashed a few yards away. I rushed out, but there was a great burst of flames and I was too late to save the two occupants. The smell of burning flesh is a memory which still haunts me.

In July the age limit for Army flyers was lowered to nineteen. I enlisted at Ithaca as a flying cadet and was soon sent to Ground School at Massachusetts Institute of Technology. For six weeks we lived on the new campus in Cambridge and drilled on the new fill where the present library and dining hall were to be built. Only on Sunday was I able to get leave for a visit to my parents or to Virginia on Beacon Hill.

In September I was sent to Kelly Field near San Antonio, Texas. The barracks and hangars were still under construction and at first we were housed in a warehouse without water or heat. Runways were not needed for the light planes we had; any field would serve. The crews were now harrowing and rolling the dirt of the landing area, formerly cotton fields, for the planes that were beginning to arrive.

Flying and the War

I soon became a flying instructor and was commissioned a Second Lieutenant in the Signal Corps. The planes we flew were the JN model designed by Curtiss, known as Jennies. All airplanes at that time were built of wood, braced by wire and covered with doped cloth. They had open cockpits in the fuselage, which was an improvement over the earlier planes in which there was no protection from the wind. Our Jennies had two cockpits with a seat in each with duplicate controls. There were no instruments, no brakes, and no parachutes. The unreliable engine was in front discharging its exhaust fumes directly into the face of the pilot in the forward seat.

Even when the engine performed well, these planes were so underpowered that it was easy to fall into a tailspin. We had been taught that it was not possible to get the Jennie out of a tailspin once it had started, but in the early fall there arrived at our airfield two barnstormers named Eddie Stinson and Phil Rader who said, "Not so." Borrowing a plane, they proceeded to demonstrate by going into a spin only 500 feet over our heads and coming out of it at a level about equal to the top of the water tower. Phil took me up to show how it was done, and that very afternoon I began experimenting by myself. Within a week we had taught all our students how to get out of a spin by pushing forward on the controls and kicking the rudder.

My students were all older than I, and when I was faced by my first class, it was obvious they thought me a patsy. The oldest and largest must have been nearly thirty and was clearly a bully. I took him up first and decided to do a loop-the-loop to scare him a bit. All my previous flying had been from the rear seat, but now I was in the instructor's seat up front. One had to dive a bit with full power to get those planes to loop. From the forward position it was easy to misjudge and I pulled up too quickly. The plane failed to climb to the top of the loop and fell back in a terrific whip-stall which must have scared me as much as it did him. I don't know what he told the rest of the

[11]

class, but they were obviously impressed and treated me with more respect.

We flyers were scornful of the non-flying officers commanding us and called them "kiwis," the Maori name for a wingless apteryx. Their orders probably came from higher brass in Washington, but often made little sense to us. At one point new cadets were arriving at the field every Saturday evening. We were each given a class of six who had never flown and told they all had to solo and be promoted to secondary training within the week; any who failed would be transferred to the infantry, which to a flyer meant being condemned as "cannon fodder."

These recruits were often airsick in that rough Texas air. One of my students started vomiting as soon as we were airborne and never stopped. By the end of the week he had never even held the controls. On Saturday afternoon I made one lap of the field with him then asked him what he wanted to do. "Solo" he replied. So I got out and turned him loose, but my knees never stopped shaking until he was on the ground again and I had certified him for secondary training. I was told he ultimately became an ace.

Another silly order came during a month when there were no new cadets arriving. Evidently it was a criterion of the efficiency of our operation to have as many flights and hours of flying per plane per day as possible. So half of us senior flyers were each assigned a plane to take up at dawn, fly around and around the field touching our wheels at every lap, but never stopping until short of gas. At noon the other half took over and flew around and around until dark.

Later in that year we began to use the Gosport system of teaching. Instead of communicating with our student by hand signals while in the air, the plane was equipped with a rubber speaking tube through which we could sometimes make out what the other chap was trying to say. At least it was an interesting guessing game and a supplement to hand signals.

In the early summer of 1918, I suffered a bitter disappointment. On the bulletin board of our Officer's Mess appeared a notice that flyers with engineering training were needed for work on the new planes now beginning to come from American assembly lines. I hadn't an engineering degree, but I had studied aerodynamics at M.I.T. under Alexander Klemin and the rudiments of design at Harvard under L. J. Johnson. Furthermore, I had often acted as test pilot of new planes, which sometimes needed radical adjustments by mechanics after assembly at the field; and I had piloted all the different makes of planes the Army had, including the "man killer" LMF. With my application for this duty overseas, I included letters of recommendation from Klemin and Johnson. Back came a rebuke with a copy of Army Regulations regarding use of civilian help in seeking promotion. I was required to write the Secretary of War explaining why I should not be subject to court-martial.

So I stayed on at Kelly Field through the hot summer months, teaching aerobatics and simulated aerial combat. Although scary, this was actually less dangerous than flying close to the ground with frequent landings at a field crowded with students in primary and secondary training. Twenty-seven of my colleagues were killed at Kelly Field during the year I taught there. One was my likeable roommate, Dick Walker, and I had the sad duty of accompanying the coffin to his home in St. Louis, comforting his weeping mother, and attending the funeral. He was killed teaching tight figure eights around a pair of pylons at low altitudes. Aerobatics are spectacular, but the only other casualty from them that I can recall was a foolhardy instructor who said that orders against stunting with an LMF were based on a myth. He tried a loop and dove into the ground. Any student of aerodynamics could have told him that the thin, cambered aerofoil of an LMF, designed for maximum lift, would be dangerous in a dive because of movement of the center of lift toward the trailing edge as the angle of incidence decreased.

Of course it can be said that many accidents of that period were due to foolhardiness and lack of discipline, but with a larger percentage of those serving in the trenches of Europe being killed in action, it was hard to get young flyers to listen to speeches on safety.

I myself had a good many narrow escapes and not just from foolhardiness. Because I was known as one of the more careful flyers, the older kiwis at our field would often invite me to fly them to some watering place or ranch where they had been asked for a weekend or a Sunday luncheon. On one such trip, I was flying a kiwi major to a beach house near Corpus Christi. I was over the middle of the city at no more than a thousand feet of altitude, studying a sketch map of the beach where we were supposed to land, when there was a sudden stream of hot oil from the engine and the propeller stopped dead. It was easy to see that a connecting rod had broken; it was sticking out from the side of the crankcase. To stretch our glide to any out-lying field or beach was obviously impossible, but there was a tiny patch of grass directly below us. With an Immelman turn and a vertical side-slip I brought the plane in between low buildings and touched down with no more damage than a broken wing skid. But the major had to send for mechanics to disassemble the plane, move it to a proper field, and install a new motor before I could fly it back to headquarters.

On another trip with a kiwi captain who wanted to visit his girl in Sabinal, we landed in a small pasture near her father's farm. There was a deep ravine on the windward end of the pasture and when we came to leave, the engine cut out just as we were becoming airborne. I kicked the plane into a terrific skid at the same time cutting the ignition. We stopped with one wing hanging over the edge of the ravine and with both tires blown, pulled off the rim by the force of the skid. With help from the farmer, we pulled the plane back, patched and rein-flated the tires, drained water from the carburetor, took off without trouble, and got back to Kelly Field while there was still enough light to land.

There were a good many other forced landings, sometimes in plowed fields or even in stands of corn. Those Jennies flew at a minimum air speed of about 40 M.P.H. and a maximum of 65. Landing in a strong wind one came down almost vertically. The engines, rarely well cared for, were run mostly with wide-open throttle. High octane gasoline was unknown and our fuel was of uncertain quality. We had to be ready for trouble. Perhaps I have had more "dead stick" landings than any man still living.

My mother had three flyers in her family to worry about and when I came home on leave, I found she was proudly displaying a three-star flag over the front door. I came home only twice during my flying career, once in January when grounded by an ear abscess, and once in November when I was transferred from Kelly Field and en route to Florida. Memory of the January visit focuses on the afternoon I took my lady-fair in the family super-six touring car to visit her married sister, Margaret Ranney, who was living in Groton during her husband's training at Fort Devens. A sudden snowstorm was the excuse for my staying overnight. After supper we walked through the fields to the village for a razor and toothbrush. The moon peeking through the clouds displayed a fairyland of snow-covered evergreens. It was a romantic setting and I was sure I was in love, but marriage seemed only an impossible dream, and my Beacon Hill sub-debutante, despite kind words and letters to her soldier, wasn't ready even to consider such a notion. Next day, when I left for Texas, she bade me Godspeed with a virginal kiss, the first I had been permitted.

Through the long hot summer, I continued to teach flying and aerial combat at Kelly Field. Then, in early November, orders came assigning me to service with the Navy. A seasoned teacher with nearly 2,000 hours of flying, I was to report at the Naval Air Base near Miami. We were told that Army airmen were going to take over coastal patrol. After a brief visit home, I arrived at the base on November 11, to find everyone celebrating the armistice. When I entered the commandant's office to present my credentials, he didn't trouble to take his feet off the desk or return my salute. He said he had no place to put any more flyers and suggested I find quarters in town, where there was plenty of amusement, and come to the base once a week to pick up any mail. He also said that if I wanted to fly, I was welcome to take any plane I found on the ramp. So I spent six weeks at the Y.M.C.A., bought an old flivver, and when we could find nothing better to do, some of us Army flyers would go to the base and delight in "wiping the eyes" of the Navy men with a scatterbrained exhibition of aerobatics which those heavy Navy sea planes had never performed before, and for which they were surely not designed.

The last time I ever piloted a plane was at Orlando, Florida, on December 18, 1918. It was the place and the day on which I was mustered out to return to college. Virginia had told me she was never going to marry a flyer, and it seemed easy to promise I would not do anything so foolish as to pilot a plane again.

CHAPTER III

⟨᠁⟩

Courtship and Marriage

I WENT back to my studies in Cambridge. Harvard made it possible to cram two years of work into one by studying around the calendar and almost around the clock. I was eager to get on my own and with this strong motivation, I became an "A" student in all six of the courses I was taking, in sharp contrast to my poor to mediocre performance as a freshman and sophomore. Then, I had been more interested in debutante parties and the social side of college life. Now, with a career in view, I was taking courses in the "practical" fields of engineering and economics. Although I could have had a war degree in June, I stayed in Cambridge until mid-December, carrying all the courses I was permitted even through the summer. In early January, I returned to Cambridge to get my degree A.B. *cum laude* in Engineering Sciences.

In this year, which I devoted so sedulously to study, I also found time to continue my courtship. I made the first proposal of marriage when Virginia and I were riding horseback together in the spring. We were on the path which circles Fresh Pond in Cambridge. Often since, she has asked me what I would have done with the horses if she had said "yes." For the rest of that spring and summer of 1919 I pressed my suit. When Virginia moved to Gateways in June, I bought for $50 an old stripped-down Hudson chassis with two bucket seats so that I could make regular visits to Weston. It had no muffler and both our parents took a dim view of the vehicle. Finally my mother offered, if I would give it up, to buy me a new Ford. In this

Model T roadster, Virginia and I spent many a summer evening parked in a country byway. I think her parents approved—at least her mother made an opportunity to question me at length and tell me what a precious girl I was seeking to marry. My own parents were uncommunicative on the subject. We were not formally engaged until September. The afternoon following her agreement to a betrothal, she suggested I take her father's Pierce Arrow touring car to the Wellesley Farms station to meet the train he took from the office. It was a 1913 model and not easy to drive. Trying to shift gears and ask his consent at the same time was too much for me. We were nearly back at Gateways before I got the car into high gear and he was laughing before I got around to the question of whether or not I could have his daughter. On her twentieth birthday, September 23rd, the engagement was announced by her parents at a small reception.

My studies at Harvard had continued through the summer. Just before the start of the fall term, the Boston police went out on strike and I joined many other college students in volunteering for emergency service. My experiences as a scab policeman were not as dramatic as were those of others, but I wasn't a bit comfortable standing alone on School Street in the midst of an angry mob with only a silver police badge pinned to my raincoat as a symbol of authority. I didn't dare to use or even to show the club and the revolver I carried under my coat. This was doubtless lucky. In those days Boston's sidewalks were mostly paved with easily extracted bricks which made handy and potent weapons. A good many of my classmates got bloody heads, but I was only hit by rotten fruit and wads of wet, muddy newspaper. When the mobs were angriest, there was usually a decent citizen who would go for reinforcements, but some of my friends still have scars to show. It was Governor Coolidge who became the hero with his demand for law and order; he called out the militia which soon restored the peace.

Courtship and Marriage

We at first thought of a late fall wedding, but the $3,000 I had saved from flight pay wasn't much security to offer a bride, and I felt obliged to accept an offer of $125 per month to become, after graduation, an employee of my father at his West Virginia properties where he was producing gas that was sold to Standard Oil. My fiancée then set the wedding date for May 15, 1920, which would give me a few months to get started in business, and her time to plan a trousseau. Also I would have a chance to find a place for us to live.

These gas properties were mostly in northern West Virginia and my father was still making a little carbon black near Spencer. He wanted me to live there and offered to buy us a house. My work was to be with the gas lines, wells, and meters throughout Roane and Calhoun Counties. There being no roads in much of this hilly country, I was expected to do a lot of walking. Spencer was a small hill town at the end of a branch railroad. I visited it in the Christmas vacation and found a tiny house in the center of town that seemed suitable, but a fortnight later, Father found a new larger one on the edge of town which he bought. It had a bathroom and lighting fixtures, but there was no water, no sewer and no electricity. I had to do most of the piping and wiring myself during the long evenings and the following October had come before it was ready. I was too busy to be lonely, living in Spencer's one hotel, the McKown, when not in the field fixing gas meters and walking pipelines.

In May, two days before our marriage, I returned to Cambridge. The wedding was in the Unitarian church in Weston and was followed by a large reception at Gateways. The minister was Palfrey Perkins, Virginia's maid of honor was her sister Linda, who later became Palfrey's wife, and my best man was my college roommate, Alec Bright. In the rehearsal it was planned that Alec would place the ring on the minister's prayerbook to be blessed before I picked it up to put on the finger of the bride. In the actual ceremony, there was an open heating register just before the altar where we stood. While blessing the ring, Palfrey let it slip from the prayerbook. It hit the middle of the register with a loud tinkle and would surely have been lost, but Alec, who had won his "H" in baseball, snatched it on the bounce and handed it to me amid peals of laughter from the whole wedding party. It was surely a good omen, for the ring has never left her finger since.

After the reception we fled in a shower of rice followed by mischievous ushers, but gave them the slip and spent our first night in Beverly Farms before catching a train for West Virginia. Although our house was far from ready when we arrived at Spencer, we did have chairs, a bed and table. Ten days later the beautiful antiques given to Virginia as wedding presents arrived by freight, and the gossips in town said, "What a shame that old man Cabot made his son start life with second-hand furniture." And when Virginia appeared at the first church supper, it was reported that she wore "yarn stockings and a homemade sweater."

It was rugged country and a rugged life for a twenty-year-old girl brought up to grace a Boston drawing room. We took our honeymoon on a horseback tour of primitive Calhoun County where the first bathtub, the first flush toilet, and the first bed sheets had yet to be seen. But it was a friendly part of the state, not given to the feuding and illicit stills which existed in the southern counties. Any farmhouse, however humble, would welcome a traveler for a meal or a night's lodging. Even when coming unannounced to a cabin which had only a dirt floor, there would be an extra straw-filled tick and patchwork quilt, where we could spend the night.

In West Virginia of sixty years ago, there were only very primitive roads; the towns had little contact with the outside world and automobile travel was practically impossible. In June of 1920 my brother Jim tried to drive a Model T Ford

Assiniboine, "Matterhorn of the Rockies," first climbed by Sir James Outram in 1901. We participated in the third ascent and in the first ascent of the adjacent Mount Magog.

Building the camp at Mount Assiniboine for Alpine Club of Canada in 1920.

Pack trip in 1923 with Chance Parry and Oliver Grimes to explore the Zion Canyon country in southern Utah.

Rain clouds over Zion Canyon. Publication of our pictures helped promote the creation of Zion and Bryce National Parks.

Approaching west rim of Zion Canyon.

Members of the party pioneering the route along the Continental Divide from Lake Louise to Mount Robson in 1924. Left to right standing: T.D.C., Henry Hall, Henry Schwab, Sir James Outram, E. V. Huntington. Sitting: Virginia, Lydia Hall, Susan Huntington.

Pack train fording the Saskatchewan River.

Castleguard Creek and Watchman Peak.

Camp at Castleguard Meadow.

Crossing the crevassed Athabasca Glacier.

Off the glacier at last.

In the shadow of Mount Robson.

At the Betemp's Hut after our climb of Monte Rosa in July 1926. Alec Bright, Virginia and the two guides.

Summit of the Dent de Requin with its unsteady slab of granite.

During the early years of our marriage, we sandwiched between business trips a week of exploration by pack and saddle horse in the mountains and deserts of southern Arizona.

When our children joined us on these desert trips they were fascinated by stories of the Lost Dutchman mine.

The Valée Blanche down which
we skied in 1957 from Col de
Geant to the Mer de Glace.

Parleying with armed bandits on Mount Popocatepetl while
climbing in Mexico before my brother's wedding.

Sierra Nevada de Santa Marta in Colombia, highest coastal range in the world, explored and climbed by members of the Cabot expedition.

Arhuaco Indians met in the Sierra Nevada de Santa Marta en route to the high peaks.

An Arhuaco Indian of the Iku tribe chewing coca leaves which he carries in a shoulder bag and fortifies with lime from the gourd in his hand.

Runabout the thirty-odd miles from Charleston to Spencer. It took him thirty hours. His car was pulled out of mudholes by oxen three different times, and the car finally caught fire pushing through the mud and burned up in the outskirts of Spencer.

The local stores carried only a few bare necessities. Nearly all one's shopping was from mail-order catalog. We bought most of our supplies, even our groceries, from Sears, Roebuck and Company in Chicago, and our only news came two days late from Parkersburg. Many of our more prosperous neighbors couldn't read or write. But even the poorest were usually members of a church and listened each Sunday to tales of the fire and brimstone that could be avoided only by a strict observance and complete acceptance of its particular creed. Cleanliness was not a part of their belief, but the Ten Commandments decidedly were, and on the whole, I think they were better observed there than in Boston.

In Spencer, before our marriage, I was occupied mostly as repairman for the meters in the nearby counties through which gas was bought and sold. I had to carry about one hundred pounds of tools and spare parts. At first, I carried these by knapsack. It was quicker to go afoot than by horseback because the roads were usually deep with mud, and on foot I could follow pipelines through the woods. But later, when my wife joined me on these trips, we always went horseback. We covered a wide area and this usually meant staying one or two nights in a primitive farmhouse with no running water. The country people had little concern for hygiene. Although we could often get eggs, the staple food was largely corn pone and sour-belly, not very appetizing or nourishing. In the six months before our wedding I lost twenty pounds.

When we moved to Charleston in the second year of our marriage, most of our trips were to the southern counties where moonshine production was the mountain people's principal cash crop. These folks were far less peaceful than the farmers around

CHAPTER IV

〜〜〜〜

Mountaineering and the Family

VIRGINIA and I returned to Boston from West Virginia a month after our wedding to be members of a bridal party of Virginia's best friend, Lydia Storer, who was marrying Henry Hall. Henry was an Alpinist and eager to introduce us to the sport. We listened to his enthusiastic description and the challenge was contagious. We agreed to join the Halls on a trip to Mount Assiniboine, in the Canadian Rockies, that was being organized by the Alpine Club of Canada. Our anticipation rose as we acquired the necessary gear, the heavy woolens, climbing boots, etc. The expedition was due to start from Banff in the first week of July, but it was a late season and the snow in the passes was still too deep for pack horses. Although we did not learn of this until our arrival at Banff, the four of us decided to press on as far as Sunshine Pass, camp there, and do our first preliminary climbing under Henry's guidance.

After a week at Sunshine, volunteers chopped out a trail to Mount Assiniboine and established a camp for the 200 club members. The Halls and I went along with them, but because of her inexperience Virginia stayed behind at Sunshine. Two days later a volunteer was needed to guide our Chinese cooks over the new trail to the Assiniboine campsite. Maybe it was love that bid Virginia to offer, but it certainly took a lot of courage for a city girl who was a complete novice at mountain travel to lead them nearly a score of miles over a faintly blazed trail.

We built our camp on the shore of the beautiful Lake Magog

that looked across at the stately and awesome Assiniboine. This "Matterhorn of the Rockies" was first climbed a few years earlier by Sir James Outram, the famous Scottish mountaineer and explorer. Today there is a permanent camp of log cabins at this lovely site built by Erling Strom.

At the Assiniboine camp we made friends with many mountaineers; some would be our companions on notable climbs in the future. On this occasion Virginia participated in the first ascent of Mount Magog and I in the third ascent of Mount Assiniboine. We gained assurance from our more experienced guides and shared in the exhilaration of great heights. This baptism admitted us as members not only of the Alpine Club of Canada but also of the American Alpine Club, the Appalachian Mountain Club, and Harvard Travellers Club. I later served the latter two as president.

These honeymoon trips to primitive Appalachia and to the wild western Rockies were quite a shocking change for a girl reared by a cultured family and educated at Miss Winsor's School for a life in Boston's high society. She took it well and soon developed a love for the rough outdoor life that she has never lost, although it competes in her affection with a love of music and art which she acquired in childhood. Our strenuous trips still continue and I think we can rightfully claim they have made us better able to withstand the thrust of time. Despite some afflictions, our apparent age belies our many years.

Our son Louis was born in August 1921. We had moved back to Boston in the summer of 1922 and a second son Tom, Jr. was born in October before we could get away for our next expedition, a horseback trip, camping in the little-known canyons of Southern Utah. We were stimulated to visit the region by reading an article in the *Saturday Evening Post* in which the author, Hal Evarts, told of being the first man to reach the West Rim of Zion Canyon. We wanted to be second. Hearing that both Zion and Bryce Canyons were being proposed for National

After a hot bath and a night in bed at the Jasper hotel, we continued northward. In three more days of riding in the flower-filled valleys, we reached Berg Lake at the foot of Mount Robson. Beside this small lake of brilliant blue dotted with icebergs from the mountain above, we pitched camp. There we stayed for two more weeks with members of the Alpine Club of Canada. We climbed many nearby peaks, but did not climb Robson. It was considered too dangerous, but it had been climbed once before in 1913 by a party led by Conrad Kain.

As my career in business prospered, we planned our first trip to Europe in 1926. The mountains were in our blood and we wanted to experience Alpinism in Switzerland where the sport originated. We left our three boys at home with a governess. We meant to begin with an Italian interlude. With three young college girls from Smith, we sailed to Sorrento and Capri and were stunned by the beauty of that part of the Italian Coast. Ashore, we continued along the Amalfi Drive in horse carts to Paestum. Then doubling back via Pompeii to Naples, we hired a touring car for the trip to Rome. From there we traveled northward through the hill towns with overnight stops at Perugia, Orvieto, and Siena. At Florence we left our new friends and went on to Lake Como where we found truth in the saying that stolen fruits are the sweetest. It was out of season and most of the great villas were unoccupied. We made some brazen visits into their gardens, saw the splendid grounds, and demonstrated total ignorance of the language when admonished in Italian by indignant gardeners. In years to come, when we were shown these same palace grounds as invited guests, we surprised our hosts by telling them of our earlier clandestine delight.

From Como we went on to Stresa on Lake Maggiore. There we hired a boat to row out to the gardens of Isola Bella which was then open to tourists. Our plan was to meet our old friend Alec Bright at Kandersteg in Switzerland. Imagine our surprise when someone in a rowboat hailed us in a disguised voice and challenged us to a race. With two oarsmen to our one, we were soon outdistanced. When allowed to catch up, there was Alec hiding in the coxswain's seat. One of the most unpredictable and amusing of traveling companions, Alec was with us for the next month, climbing and skiing the mountains and glaciers of the Bernese and Valais Alps of Switzerland.

The morning after our chance meeting he grabbed my train tickets to Brig, rushed to turn them in and announced he had hired a touring car to take us *over* the Simplon instead of through that miserable railroad tunnel. When we finally reached Brig, he rushed off to buy a pair of climbing boots and missed the train to Kandersteg. By the time we caught up with each other, he had the whole town agog by riding a bicycle backward down the main street while sitting on the handlebars.

We had several good climbs in the Bernese Alps, the best of which were of the Balmhorn and the Altels. We climbed after a night in a tiny inn on the Gemmi Pass. In this inn Alec's scant knowledge of German and his arbitrary use of "du" and "dir" had a chambermaid rushing off with her face in her apron.

From Kandersteg we hiked for two days over the snow-filled passes to Murren. There Alec managed to miss the train again, but ran down the mountainside to overtake it at Lauterbrunnen. Continuing to the hotel at Jungfraujoch we met Albert Mc-Carthy, an indomitable naval hero who was making a whirlwind climbing tour of the Alps. Albert kept up a running battle with the hotel management over the question of drinking water. He insisted that he wouldn't drink carbonated water from bottles and the management insisted that snow water would give him dire diseases. It ended when McCarthy brought into the dining room the large china pitcher from the washstand in his bedroom and poured a drink for each and every American he could find in the room.

Next day we climbed the Jungfrau and returned to the hotel where we hired skis for a descent of the Aletsch Glacier. After a night in the Concordia Hut, we continued to a hotel near the Mariellen See from which we mailed our skis for just a few pennies back to the hotel at Junfraujoch where we had hired them. Continuing afoot into the Rhone Valley at Fiesch, we made a railroad connection to Zermatt.

Eager to try the Matterhorn, we employed some guides for the ascent. No other party had yet been up that year. The guides took us on several lesser climbs while awaiting fair weather, and after testing our competence we ascended the Matterhorn via the Hörnli Ridge. It was a slow trip because of snow. We took twenty-four hours from our 1:00 A.M. start at the Hörnli Hut to reach the summit and return to the hotel down in the valley—quite a *tour de force* for Virginia, a mother of three. Before leaving Zermatt, we also climbed Monte Rosa to the Dufourspitze, the highest peak in Switzerland, and made a ski ascent of the Breithorn.

The wooden skis of that period were not equipped with metal edges and, for our part, we were not very competent skiers. On our descent from the Breithorn summit our route led along the brink of the icefall abreast of the Kleine Matterhorn. Tongues of ice dropped to the Theodule Glacier below. Suddenly my wife's skis got sliding sideways, and in an instant she disappeared over the edge of the 600-foot drop. The steep icy slope obscured the view and there was no chance to see what disaster had befallen her. Fritz Ogi, our guide, cached his skis and started to chop steps down the icefall, but it would obviously take him an hour or more to reach the glacier below. With a yell, Alec started skiing like mad down the gentler slope to the west that we had climbed before dawn. Schussing the last quarter mile we soon came upon her prostrate body. She was crying—unhurt but mad at herself and frightened by what might have happened. The slide over the icefall had scraped off much of her outer clothing, but the gradually lessening slope broke her fall and saved her from injury.

Mountaineering and the Family

It was too late in the season to attempt the Haut Route by ski to Chamonix; for the time being we had had enough. So we took the train down the Rhone to Martigny and an electric trolley car from there over the mountains. In the outskirts of Martigny we passed through an orchard of ripe cherries. I began to gather them through the open windows of the car. To get more, Alec climbed through the window onto the car roof. He harvested a capful of the fruit but was soon apprehended by the motorman who stopped the car and surely would have arrested him had he shown any sign of understanding the language.

At Chamonix the guide, Marcel Bozon, frequently took us climbing in the Aiguilles. These needles of hard crystalline granite afford some of the world's most famous ascents. We made a traverse of the Grepon. Swinging to the Mummery Crack we could get toes and fingers into that narrow fissure for the ascent of the sheer face high above the Mer de Glace. Later, we were joined by English friends for the ascent of the Dent de Requin. To reach this we walked up the glacier and spent a short night in the new Requin Hut, where we slept fourteen on a shelf so crowded we had to roll over in unison. We were up before daylight for the long, precipitous climb culminating in the difficult over-hang of the flat slab which forms the summit. I still shiver when I think of the scare I had when, exhausted from the struggle to pull myself over the edge of the slab, I rose to shake the congratulatory hand of Bozon who led the rope. As I took a step toward him that great platform slab of rock tilted a good six inches under my advancing weight. I was so flustered that I could hardly obey Bozon's instructions as to where I had to put my weight so that the next man on the rope would have the identical experience.

This was our first expedition involving really hazardous technical climbing. Several of our mountaineering friends were killed in climbing accidents at about this time, and we concluded that what we gained in self-confidence and exhilaration hardly

[29]

justified the risk of a fatality. We kept up our love of mountain hiking and travel, but among true Alpinists we are considered renegades.

During our sojourn at Chamonix we stayed at a *pension* in an old-fashioned high-studded room that contained a large wardrobe made of golden oak. The wardrobe had a carved frieze extending above its front. During this time France was experiencing a decline in the value of the franc to one-tenth the level prior to World War I. In the country districts one could buy produce for ridiculously low prices when figured in dollars. Alec bought several yard-long loaves of bread and a great cheese as big as a cartwheel which he carried home on the handlebar of his bicycle. We kept it on top of the high wardrobe, and consumed only a minor portion of it during our stay. Only when we reached London did we remember the cheese and wondered how long it would remain hidden on top of the wardrobe!

I was once warned by a teacher that I should not marry a Boston girl because we Bostonians are slightly crazy from inbreeding. Well, Virginia and I have not yet discovered a common ancestor; our children are healthy, and we are a family noted for our togetherness. It was only a matter of time before our children began accompanying us on less rigorous expeditions. Our three sons, Louis, Tommie, and Rob born in 1921, 1922, and 1924, were followed by a daughter Linda in 1928 and after a gap of almost fifteen years, by Ned in 1943. All had begun to ride, ski, canoe, and camp with us while they were still quite small. I often talked about my youthful camping in southern Arizona and I was naturally eager to show off my capability as a horse wrangler and packer. On several occasions we managed to sandwich between business trips a week or more of exploration in the mountains and canyons of the lovely desert country I had known as a boy. My old friend, Major Brady, and ranchers such as Tex Barclay and Charlie Weeks were good enough to loan us horses and pack outfits and we would go off, unguided, and often into unfamiliar territory. In those days Arizona was a romantic part of the world. If we ever met a cowhand or prospector he would regale us with tales of fierce Indians, wild gun battles, lost mines, and discovering skeletons of pioneers who had died of thirst. The automobile and irrigation of the valley deserts has changed most of this, but the pioneering days were then still well within the memory of a man in middle age.

My wife became skilled at cooking biscuits in a Dutch oven with dried dung as fuel, and I at tracking and catching the horses each morning. In desert country horses will wander for miles and finding them in the morning takes lots of horse-sense. February and March were our preferred months. At that time of year we could expect a bit of rain to produce grass for the horses and a gorgeous show of wild flowers for us.

This was the land of the Lost Dutchman Mine, a favorite of many writers including Erle Stanley Gardner. I never knew the Dutchman; he died before my first visit to Arizona. But most of my early friends knew him and each had his own theory about the mine. We still speculate as to whether it was buried by an earthquake or whether this lonely German prospector was clever enough to hide all clues so that it can never be rediscovered. There is no doubt he found a rich lode of gold in those hills, but when he died in Phoenix the secret of its location died with him.

When our children joined us on these desert trips, they were fascinated by such stories and they learned a lot about camping, horses, and the wild western mountains. Our three older boys all accompanied us on Arizona pack trips in the 1930's.

Linda was with us on the last of these trips in 1941. We were lucky in the weather; the rains had just ended, the flooded rivers were subsiding, and the wild flowers were never more beautiful. The air was clear as crystal, and we could see a hundred miles from the mountain tops. Automobile roads had hardly intruded into these mountains then, and views from the heights into the valleys were probably much as they appeared to early pioneers. Since then the valleys have become filled with houses and the air is constantly yellow with pollution.

On Christmas Eve, 1942, our Army son, Rob, was overseas; but our Navy sons, Louis and Tommie, got home in time to hang stockings over the hearth with their sister and parents. They were a bit curious about a tiny stocking at the end of the row and you can probably imagine their silent amazement when these veterans learned that their middle-aged parents were planning to present them with a little brother or sister in the early summer. Ned, our youngest, was born the following July and he was named after my partner, Ned Billings, who was reported missing in action when the heavy cruiser *Quincy* was sunk in the Solomon Islands.

Son Ned was not quite six when we took him on his first pack trip with horses. By then we had the Bar NI Ranch in Colorado. Alec Bright came with us and shared a tent with Ned. Alec was still unmarried. Although a famous athlete, he wasn't noted as a horseman, whereas Ned had ridden from the age of three. They were a great combination and each learned a lot about mountain travel. We took them over the top of the Sangre de Christo Range. This was one of the most notable of dozens of pack trips in the region. Ned grew up to become a skilled horse wrangler and packer under our tutelage and has frequently taken his own family and friends on trips in those same mountains. Many of our grandchildren now visit at this ranch and go on pack trips with us.

Ned was fourteen when he accompanied me on what proved a rather frightening expedition in the Alps. Our guide was Alex Perren from Zermatt; Horace and Alec Bright had skied with him the previous year and had given him the highest rating. I had long wanted to ski the glaciers and passes between Zermatt and Chamonix, called the Haut Route, but Ned could not leave school until early June and when we reached Zermatt we found that the warm spring had left insufficient snow for our undertaking. As an alternative, our guide suggested we ski across the Theodule Pass to Cervinia in Italy, motor to Courmayeur, take the funicular to Col de Geant, and ski down to Chamonix via the Vallée Blanche and Mer de Glace.

At Col de Geant we met some Italian guides giving skiing lessons on the glacier who told us that no one had been down the Vallée Blanche for several weeks and that to attempt it would be foolish as the recent warm spell had opened the crevasses and melted the snow bridges. But guide Alex, with his Swiss scorn for all things Italian, was impelled to give it a try. After all, we were good skiers, well-equipped with rope and ice axes. At each crevasse we looked for a place to cross, then with the rope belayed to axes driven into the snow, each schussed across the slender bridge over the yawning gulf of blue ice. To retrace our path by climbing up such perilous spans was unthinkable and one couldn't help but wonder if we were not heading for an impasse. As we descended, the snow became softer and scarcer, the bridges scantier and riskier, and the crevasses more frequent. Nearly down to the Mer de Glace, we came to a wide crevasse with no bridge at all. We were stranded on a narrow shelf of ice with no visible means of escape. The fragile bridge by which we had reached it surely would not support a climber. My heart sank to think I had brought my young son into such a predicament.

Alex unroped, took crampons from his knapsack and, leaving skis and pack with us, set out along the shelf and was soon out of sight. He had told us not to unrope and not to move. Morbid thoughts soon filled our minds. Had he dropped into a crevasse? When would we be missed and how could a rescue team find us or ever reach us if we were spotted by a plane?

It started to rain. An hour passed. It seemed forever. Perhaps it was only an hour and a half when we heard a hail from below.

It was Alex climbing to us with crampons up the edge of a slab of ice. He had found a way to the *bergschrund* which he would need our help to cross. With the aid of the rope we carried our skis down the hazardous ice slope to the lip of the *bergschrund*. Below us, wedged in the twelve-foot-wide crack, was a sliver of ice leading to the opposite wall. This was a vertical cliff of blue ice perhaps twenty feet high that was surmounted by a black rock face leading up into the clouds. It was an awesome place, but we soon had our ice axes well planted for a belay and lowered Alex to the sliver which he crossed to the cliff. This he attacked with mighty axe strokes providing foot holds and hand holds in that vertical face. Meanwhile we tended the rope and belay, shivered in our wet clothes, and prayed he would not slip lest we not be strong enough to hold and both be pulled into the dark abyss below. It must have taken another hour for him to gain a ledge in the rocks above and drive a piton into the rock to belay us. First, the three pairs of skis must be hauled to the ledge, then we each made the difficult climb to join him. Carrying our skis on a traverse along the rocks, looking down into that awful mouth of ice, was just as difficult, but it wasn't long before we descended to the gentler ice of the Mer de Glace. We skied down in heavy rain to the cog railroad for the short trip to Chamonix.

In the hotel, we had just sent our clothes to the furnace room to dry and were putting on fresh underwear when there was a comic performance of a parade in the street below our window. For a better view we draped towels around our bare legs and went out into the yard. There was a shouted "Hi, Tom," from a fifth-floor window and who should it be but my Harvard class-mate and neighbor, Carl Fuller and his wife Dorothy. They had come to Chamonix for some climbing of the famous Aiguilles. When our clothes were dry, we all had dinner together. Carl got into a discussion with Alex about the Zmutt Arete of the Matterhorn which they climbed together a few days later.

Mountaineering and the Family

I mention this dinner at which Carl and Alex met because a year later Alex wrote me at home and told of a tragic accident in which he had lost his leg, fractured while guiding a French client on the Sudwand of the Obergabelhorn. In the eighteen hours before help arrived, the leg had frozen, requiring amputation. The Brights, Carl Fuller, and I all wanted to help and when we learned that he had been offered a loan by a Zurich bank to build a hotel in Zermatt if he could find $40,000 of additional equity, immediately we sent him the money. The loan was repaid, and the thriving Hotel Alex has made him a millionaire. He hired as his manager a charming girl from Vienna, later married her, and they are now the proud parents of four handsome children. Despite his false leg he still skis and occasionally even teaches a ski class.

Our love of the mountains has continued, but we are sorry that Alpinism today has come to imply the ascent of the most difficult routes, spectacular faces of rock and ice, and the use of fancy hardware. Climbing mountains does have merit as a way to build physique and muscular coordination. It develops confidence and responsibility and trains one to control irrational fears. But we have concluded that these merits are outweighed by the risks. There are other sports of equal merit where the penalty for a mistake is less than fatal. One can learn to control acrophobia, or the irrational fear of heights sometimes misnamed vertigo, by limiting one's climbing to cliffs where a stout rope can be tended should one slip. But admittedly, this removes the real peril and limits the challenge, and these are essential elements in the fascination with the sport. The mountains have a lure. There is a mystery one must dare to solve, a compulsion to predict the difficulties one will encounter. From afar, one considers the various routes, trying to imagine the best leads, the surest path. And if one succeeds, there is a satisfaction that cannot be denied, especially if you're the first to do it. But each success adds to the challenge, and each challenge augments the danger, for with each successful ascent the Alpinist feels the compulsion to try something yet more difficult. We have had far too many friends and acquaintances who have thus gone on, always developing their climbing skill by seeking ever more difficult challenges until at last a fatal slip ends a promising career. In addition the modern trend is clearly aimed at seeking routes possible only with elaborate hardware. It is not for us.

Exploration has replaced Alpinism, leading us to mountains where less climbing technique is demanded. For instance, while in Mexico for my brother Jack's wedding, I climbed Ixtacihuatl and Popocatepetl with Henry Hall and Walter Wood. But this experience turned out to involve bandits more than mountain hazards. We were warned beforehand to leave all our money and valuables in the hotel in Mexico City. This provided some comfort when we returned to find our camp occupied by armed bandits. The job of negotiating fell to me, and I succeeded in keeping our cameras by explaining in my fractured Spanish that the numbers were registered which rendered them unsaleable. We did lose all our cooking utensils and much of our equipment but felt lucky to have escaped with our lives.

We got back to the city only just in time for the wedding, where I acted as best man. It was a gala affair attended by most members of the diplomatic corps. Jack, who is four years younger than I, and his wife, Elizabeth, have had a career as diplomats which has taken them far afield. It has been our privilege to visit them at the many embassies where they have presided.

As health and business permitted, our explorations culminated in further trips to Canada and Latin America. Late in 1929 we were invited to visit and photograph a herd of caribou reported on top of Table Mountain. This is the central wilderness area of the Gaspe Peninsula near Quebec. The trip turned into a minor disaster because, unprepared for the distance and climate, we did not bring a proper food supply or shelter. It started snowing, and, inadequately protected from the cold, I had to light a fire. But getting the wet kindling wood to burn was not easy and I had to kneel so long in the snow that a painful knee inflammation resulted and I couldn't walk. While the rest of the party went up the mountain to see the caribou, Virginia and I got ourselves to a deserted ranger's cabin. In a dark corner we found an abandoned telephone and a coil of bare wire. Climbing a tree, I hitched it to the pole line and could hear dim voices. But it was the perseverance of my wife that finally brought relief. She spent the entire evening cranking the phone and repeating, "mon mari a blessé le genou." A warden with a horse arrived at 2:00 A.M. and carried me out of the woods.

It took several weeks to cure my knee and the exposure gave my wife pneumonia. Her impaired health lasted into the winter. We wanted a tropical holiday. This was at a time when Jack was chargé d'affaires in Santo Domingo and he asked us down for a visit. We naturally accepted, decided to go by boat, and being curious Yankees, we studied the terrain in atlases and encyclopedias before leaving. All, including Webster's Dictionary, mentioned a mountain, the Loma Tina, as 10,300 feet high in the southern part of the Dominican Republic. Nowhere in the mountaineering journals could we find proof that it had ever been climbed. So, hoping for a first ascent, we brought along camping and mountaineering equipment.

We found Santo Domingo a primitive city of adobe houses with mud streets and open sewers, quite a contrast to the modern buildings and luxurious hotels there today. Loma Tina, as located on the maps, was in country of few inhabitants. Inquiries revealed no one who had even seen the mountain. By all accounts, none of the mountains in that vicinity exceeded 4,500 feet. To confirm this, we took a three-day camping trip with horses into the region, climbing several of the highest ridges. It was an exciting trip. We had never experienced a tropical rain forest or seen its many animals and forbidding jungle flora. We passed close to the spectacular Jimenoa Falls, forded mountain streams, and climbed the steep hillsides with horses so small that our feet barely cleared the ground. From the 4,500 foot ridges we could see no high mountain that could possibly be Loma Tina.

We left Santo Domingo in a hired car with driver and drove over very primitive dirt roads to the north coast of the island where we visited the ruined palace of King Christof at San Souci and rode by mule up the steep track to his impregnable fort built to defy Napoleon. This enormous mass of masonry high on the cliffs, surrounded by hundred-foot vertical walls, contains rooms for a thousand soldiers and a year's supply of stores. It is topped by a parade ground where troops could drill. Below are bastions with gun ports for a hundred cannon. Stories are told of the frightful torture used to maintain unswerving discipline. One hundred slaves would be given the task of hauling a cannon up those awesome slopes and the first to falter would be lashed to death. A British admiral sent to negotiate a treaty against Napoleon describes seeing a demonstration by Christof of the valor of his troops—he ordered a platoon to march over the edge of the 500-foot vertical drop from the parade ground. Not a man faltered.

No wonder there have been more than a hundred revolutions in Haiti since those days.

At Cape Haitian we stayed with the American Consul and from there we went to Port-au-Prince, following roads that were being improved with the assistance of the United States Marines who had occupied the country since 1916. At Port-au-Prince we boarded a cruise ship for Panama. The luxurious liner was a sharp contrast to the Haitian poverty prevailing in those days. From Panama we flew across the isthmus to Panama City—Virginia's first plane ride. Before continuing our journey by banana boat to Santa Marta, we spent a restless night listening to the howling monkeys of Barro Colorado Island in Gatun Lake. When this lake was formed as part of the Panama Canal, great numbers of wild animals took refuge on its high ground. Professor Barbour persuaded Harvard to establish a station for research in animal behavior on this new island. It was a unique experience to spend a day and a night among these hordes of animals in their native forest guided by the naturalists studying there.

Upon our arrival at Santa Marta we were met by Tom and Mary Bradshaw who invited us to stay with them. Tom was local manager for United Fruit Co. and showed us some of the techniques used in growing bananas and coffee. But our particular interest lay in the high mountains and the Arhuaco Indians living in the scattered villages above the farms and without contact with civilization. The snow-covered summits were not visible from the seaport, but with Tom's help we arranged a visit to the coffee *finca* of Orlando Flye high in the foothills. There we were permitted to bivouac on the 10,000-foot ridge of his property and at dawn had an unforgettable view of great glaciers and icefalls descending into the tropical forest from the snow-capped peaks of the main range. These rise nearly 19,000 feet only twenty miles from the Caribbean shore. By any standard they are the highest coastal mountains in the world.

We could find little local knowledge of the interior of the range or of its primitive inhabitants. We resolved to explore. On our return to the Bradshaws' we rebooked our departure on a later sailing and cabled home not to expect us for a fortnight.

To organize a trip into this jungle wilderness wasn't easy. Tom insisted that we go with armed guards and pack mules, and these accompanied us on a two-day trip to the first Indian village, a collection of small, thatched huts clustered around the larger hut of the *cacique*. We were ushered into the single, smoke-filled room to meet the *cacique* and his council who were lying on mats in a drugged stupor from chewing coca leaves for-tified with lime dipped from gourds. They were not unfriendly but we had difficulty in communicating and learned little about their life.

Beyond this village the trail was too steep to ride. We left our guard with the mules while four of us, including my wife, went up through the rain forest hoping to locate a good ap-proach to the highest peaks. We never reached the snow but camped at about 10,000 feet. Before dawn next day I left camp alone, with a flashlight, and went above 12,000 feet but had no view of the glaciers or summits. We returned to port just in time for the trip home.

On returning to New York and Boston, I found more infor-mation about the range, but there were no adequate maps. As to the height of the summits, estimates ran from 16,300 feet by the British Admiralty, to 27,000 feet by Alexander von Hum-boldt.

My assertion as to the non-existence of Loma Tina was ac-cepted by geographers, and it has disappeared from newer maps and gazetteers. Apparently it first appeared on a map published in Santo Domingo in 1854, based on surveys of Sir Robert Schom-burgk, British Consul to the new Republic. One must suppose that two separate summits, misidentified as one, resulted in the false triangulation.

Nine years elapsed before I had the chance to return to San-ta Marta to explore, climb, and map that unique group of moun-tains. During that time, I read all I could find about the region and talked with various naturalists who had worked in the lower hills of the range. In early 1939 I managed to find time from my business responsibilities, and with nine days to prepare, got together and equipped an expedition under the sponsorship of the American Geographical Society. Walter Wood was in charge of surveying and map making, Frank Notestein joined up as our geologist, Anderson Bakewell as naturalist, and Henry Hall as mountaineer. Aided by aerial photographs, we made our approach, not through the rain forests of the coast as before, but from Valle Dupar south of the range where there were good trails up to the highest pastures built by members of the Iku tribe inhabiting those high valleys.

Walter and Henry had climbed with me before, and all of the party were familiar with ice axe and crampons. Henry and I flew to Barranquilla on one of the first commercial intercontinental flights, while the others traveled by steamer. On our arrival in Colombia, we soon learned from German residents that a group of German mountaineers had been in the Santa Marta mountains for the previous three weeks and had just left for Europe. We found that they had enlisted as a climbing companion a local resident of Swiss-Italian descent named Praolini. We sought him out and were told that they had made a first ascent of the central summit of the highest massif, but Praolini thought the unclimbed eastern summit might be higher. We persuaded him to join our group for a try on it. Incidentally, I don't think any account of this German expedition has been published, presumably because all the members became involved in the war before anything could be recorded. When the freighter with the rest of our group on deck approached the dock in Santa Marta, we shouted across the water, "Martha is no longer virgin!" Doubtless the message was misinterpreted by the other passengers.

For the older members of the party our climb from Valle Dupar was too sudden. We oldsters (I was then forty-two) had not enough time to get acclimated and were stricken with hypoxia. Only Wood, Bakewell, and Praolini reached the summit. This was the eastern peak which has since been named Colon. Whether its summit is higher than that of the central peak now named Bolivar is uncertain. Both peaks are crowned with a snow cornice which varies from year to year. As seen from Colon when looking with an Abney level, the two peaks appeared as about the same height.

We older members who never got higher than 15,000 feet found our reward in the magnificent mountain scenery and the unique flora and fauna. Even more notable were the Indians we met. The tribes in those mountains have had little contact with white men. They pasture sheep and cattle on the high slopes and grow a little corn lower down by burning patches of forest to create a field. We were able to trade mirrors, beads, knives, and trinkets for some minor supplies and the hire of bullocks to help carry equipment to successively higher camps. Their customs and culture have recently been studied by my young friend, James Billipp of Jaffrey, New Hampshire, and it was my privilege to help Harvard obtain the artifacts he collected.

We were three weeks in the field collecting, surveying, and climbing. A fine Swiss theodolite loaned to us by the Society enabled us to triangulate the main peaks from baselines we established, and with time signals from Washington we made an accurate determination of latitude and longitude. Later we flew over the range in a trimotor Ford plane using a Fairchild survey camera to fill in the topography. Our published maps and descriptions have inspired scores of subsequent climbing expeditions to these mountains and now all of the major peaks have been climbed more than once. The Colombian government expressed its gratitude by naming one of the minor summits of this great range in my honor.

Accounts of this expedition have appeared in *The Geographical Review, The Alpine Journal,* and *Appalachia.*

That was my last real exploration, but Virginia and I have made countless trips since to remote parts of the world. We have continued to make pack trips with horses especially in the Colorado mountains. My skill at packing horses and tying diamond hitches taught me by Major Brady when I was at school in Arizona led to a recent incident of great embarrassment sixty years later. The blame is mine.

David and Peggy Rockefeller had invited us with Mac and

Sheila Perkins to visit them at the Rockefeller ranch in the Teton Mountains of Wyoming. While there, we went on a short pack trip. It was deluxe, with far more heavy equipment than Virginia and I were accustomed to. There were about eight pack horses and three guides to do the packing. Of course we enjoyed the luxury, but it did slow the trip to have so much baggage. It may have been my impatience or perhaps my vanity that led to the embarrassment. The three professionals were working as a team, packing the horses at a leisurely rate, one at a time. Our riding horses had been saddled, ready to leave for more than an hour, when I remarked that if three horses were packed at the same time using a one-man diamond hitch we would have long been under way. It was said *sotto voce*, for I meant no offense to the pros, but Peggy promptly announced that on the next horse, the last as it happened, I would demonstrate how to pack a horse with a one-man diamond. There was no denying the challenge. So, as the horse was led up, I took off my jacket, spat on my hands and went to it at a pace consistent with a real competition rather than as a daily chore—and that horse was packed in half the usual time. Fortunately the cowboy guides had the sense to take the matter as a jest, and showed no wounded pride. All day they jeered at the horse for being so docile, and whipped or prodded it in unsuccessful attempts to get it to buck off its pack. But we reached home with the pack still in place.

The pleasure we have had from horseback trips, especially those in the wilderness of our western mountains, have brought a recreation far more important in our lives than other sports. Competitive games have had little appeal. The hills, the sea, the streams, the woods, and the snowy slopes have been our inspiration. We hope our grandchildren will continue to be able to enjoy these country pleasures and will have the satisfaction of being able to cope with Nature in her changing moods. It is beyond our belief that a world without wilderness would permit an equal sense of fulfillment.

CHAPTER V

꒰ ᘛ ꒱

Cabot and Carbon Black

SOOT was used by the ancients as a pigment. During the early nineteenth century lampblack, made by burning coal tar products, was the preferred soot used in printing ink, but carbon black, made by impinging a gas flame against a plate or channel of steel, proved superior, and after 1870 it gradually replaced lampblack. However, it was not until the discovery during World War I that carbon black had remarkable properties for reinforcing rubber products that the carbon black industry grew to formidable dimensions.

My father started making carbon black from natural gas in western Pennsylvania soon after his graduation from Harvard in 1882. His business remained very small in its early years, but in 1899 he built a larger plant in West Virginia where unmarketable gas had been discovered while drilling for oil. He kept no accounts other than a checkbook, but the business must have been profitable for he was able to support his family with some measure of comfort. Much gas, a natural adjunct of the oil, was wasting into the skies and it could be bought for practically nothing. There were also opportunities to buy gas lands and producing wells at very low cost and these proved quite valuable with the increased demand for gas in World War I. When he joined the Navy in 1917, he had no one to look after his business; there were no employees in the office or plant with an education beyond the eighth grade. He was forced to shut down most of his carbon black production, but was still able to sell the gas to sup-

port the expanding pipe lines supplying steel mills and other industries at a price far higher than that at which he was buying
gas.

Despite the income tax established before the war, he had no
books from which income could be determined. His business was
a sole proprietorship. His entire office consisted of a clerk and a
stenographer, both males, neither of whom knew double-entry
bookkeeping. Receipts and expenditures were listed, but no dis-
tinction made between current expenses and capital expenditures. The only clue to costs or earnings was his bank balance
plus his innate sense of changes in the value of his properties.

With the proprietor in the Navy, the business languished.
When I and my older brother, Jim, came to work for our father
after the First World War, things were in a dreadful mess. Jim
went to West Virginia to take charge. Before Christmas of 1919,
my father sent me to Spencer to investigate leakage in the gas
lines. In a few hours I wired home that in the first half mile of
a line I counted 131 leaks that I could hear without stooping,
and that one of them had blown off my hat! This and similar
reports convinced my father that his boys could cope with business as well as technical problems.

In January, I had to return to Harvard for a week to get my
degree. Then, at Jim's suggestion, I went to Erie and Pittsburgh to study gas measurement, particularly the new orifice
meters. I found there was a discrepancy of nearly ten percent
between meters of Standard Oil and our meters made by American Meter Company. As a result of questions about this difference, Mr. Howell Cooper, chief engineer of Standard Oil, agreed
to meet me at the site where we delivered gas in the remote
town of Grantsville, West Virginia. It took some persuasion
to convince Mr. Cooper of my view that the difference was in-
herent to the mathematics of orifice meters, but when convinced,
he hired a physicist to study the problem. As a result of this,
Standard Oil discontinued the manufacture of meters. My claim

of meter inaccuracy, plus the claim that the measurement was not consistent with the interpretation of an earlier contract, resulted in our receiving a check from Standard Oil for more than $100,000, probably more than the business had ever earned in a single year.

With this impressive beginning, my responsibilities followed fast. The more important of these were related to the office rather than the field, which was Jim's province. I was soon taking a night course in accounting and handling the problem of unpaid taxes.

On his return from service in the Navy, my father had engaged a young lawyer, Merrill Griswold, to deal with his income tax delinquency. For too long the tax collectors had been told: "Young man, income is only a matter of opinion. No mere bookkeeper who hasn't seen my property can say whether I am richer or poorer at the end of the year than at the beginning. No sane man buys tangible property expecting it to depreciate in value." Merrill finally had to appeal to me to hire an accountant. With the help of the Lybrand accounting firm I went about the difficult task of preparing accounts from the meager checkbook and letter file records of the previous eight years. First we needed opening entries as of March 1, 1913, when the income tax became effective. This meant inventories and appraisals by engineers based largely on guesses as to when each item had been acquired. At the same time we had to establish business systems and policies, find competent personnel and run the day-to-day business such as it was.

The first members of management with a college education to join us were Winslow Duerr and Edmund Billings. Ned was my college roommate and had been trained as a research chemist. Winslow was hired by my father because a neighbor in Cambridge had asked his advice about a daughter marrying an impecunious school teacher named Duerr earning only $100 per month. When my father heard that the young man had graduated from Harvard with an A.B. in chemistry *summa cum laude*, he immediately offered to hire him at $200 and I was told to put him to work.

At first both Jim and I lived in West Virginia. He had an office in Charleston with a secretary-clerk and tried to stop the wastage in the properties while I assisted him in problems of management and gas measurement from my home in Spencer. Both of us made frequent visits to Boston. In early 1921, after I had lived fifteen months in Spencer, my father decided to go with my mother on a world tour. Jim moved to Boston and I to Charleston. By June, 1922 the problems of accounting and tax delinquency had become so critical that Virginia and I moved to Boston and Jim returned to Charleston. My father got home that summer and in the fall moved to Washington to pursue his interest in aviation. This left the leadership to me. The business had become profitable. The tax claims were settled, and we had an accountant, Jim Kennedy, who kept track of earnings. At our suggestion, my father decided to incorporate the business. All 1,600 shares of the stock of Godfrey L. Cabot, Inc., were issued him for assets as of October 1, 1922. Until his death forty years later, he never acknowledged that anyone but he alone could make decisions regarding the business. However, he rarely quarrelled with the decisions we made. He had no interest in accounting and still considered figures for assets, earnings, or depreciation merely the subjective opinion of a bookkeeper with no real knowledge of properties. He held the presidency of the company until he was in his nineties.

Before he left for Washington, my father was persuaded by a promoter to help finance the Salem Gasoline Company, which built a plant to extract liquids from the natural gas in Salem, West Virginia. I was made treasurer and kept the accounts. When it became apparent that the promoter was incompetent at running the plant, Duerr was put in charge.

Billings was made sales manager in Boston. We had little of

our own product to sell, but contracts were made to act as general sales agent of carbon black plants in Louisiana and Montana. Soon we were acquiring a financial interest in some of these plants and taking an increasing responsibility for their management as well.

With carbon black selling at high prices and in short supply in 1922, the industry added many new plants. The producers whose black we sold expanded their plants, but little of the increased production reached the market in time to benefit from the high prices. By mid-1923 the price of carbon black had dropped until ordinary grades were selling below cost. Many producers found themselves in financial trouble, and by the end of that year there was talk of mergers. The talks lasted months, and by 1925 nearly all of the independent producers in the industry had merged to form United Carbon Company, now a division of Ashland Oil. United Carbon was second in size to Columbian Carbon, now a division of Cities Service, which had been formed before the turn of the century. The sales agents, Binney & Smith of New York, were handling some eighty percent of the world's carbon black. It was a clear monopoly and potentially dangerous. Sure enough, in September of 1925 that firm and its principals in Louisiana, whose product we handled, announced they were raising prices by sixty percent. We immediately made plans to produce black ourselves.

Most of the world's carbon black was then produced in the large gas field near Monroe, Louisiana. There was no other market for the gas there at the time, but the producers could have withheld the gas in the expectation that pipe lines to distant cities would provide a market. This prospect kept gas prices there above the price of casinghead gas in the oil fields of Texas, which came with the oil and couldn't be withheld. This gas, for lack of a market, was wasting into the air. When crossing Texas in 1921, I had seen the huge flares at plants extracting gasoline from this casinghead gas. Duerr and I went to test the residue gas from some of these plants and to determine the possibility of making carbon black from this waste product.

We went from Fort Worth to west Texas by automobile, testing gas at scores of plants. We used the crudest of apparatus for our estimates, only a tin pie-plate, a short length of rubber tubing, a slotted tip, and some small paper envelopes. We would burn the gas, holding the pie-plate with pliers above the flame for ten minutes, then the soot was scraped into a marked envelope to be weighed later at a drug store. The relative weights correlated very closely with the relative productivity in a commercial plant. Based on such crude tests, we built eight carbon black plants in Texas and one in Oklahoma between 1925 and 1930. All of these were "channel" plants, built to our design by our own employees. The gas supplies were based on contracts which I negotiated and personally drafted. Thus, as my father had many years earlier, we became scavengers, manufacturing a useful product from a raw material that was being wasted. Until the Great Depression these plants were very profitable.

All carbon black in those days was still being made by collecting the soot which formed when a gas flame impinged on a metal surface. This usually meant steel plates or channels about eight inches wide suspended over rows of many small flames each issuing from a slotted tip about the size of a child's finger. The plants were crude and the process wasteful, for only about three percent of the elemental carbon in the gas was saved. No better method had been discovered to make a product suitable for reinforcing rubber or making proper printing ink. The product of this impingement process is usually called channel black to distinguish it from the furnace black made today.

A channel black plant consists of many long, narrow sheet-metal sheds, each with a table of parallel steel channels suspended flat side down a few inches apart. The channels are mounted on wheels so that they move lengthwise a few feet, and the black is scraped into hoppers as they move. In 1925, the traditional plants were bolted together by blacksmiths and arranged in units of about thirty sheds. Power was provided by a central gas engine through a series of shafts, belts, pulleys, chains, sprockets, racks, and pinions. If anything broke, it was necessary to shut down and cool off the whole unit in order to make a repair. We were the first to bring engineering training to the industry.

I would go by train to Texas many times each year to sort things out with Duerr, to plan the next step of our expansion and to negotiate new gas contracts. These I personally drafted on the spot, working far into the night. Then on the long train trip home, I drew plans for each plant, simple pencil plans on an ordinary block of paper, and from these I prepared a bill of materials which could be ordered on my arrival in Boston. We were our own engineers; we made no blueprints, only rough sketches which the untrained construction foreman could follow. On our own initiative we designed our plants with individual electric motors driving each pair of sheds. Instead of small groups of sheds around a central power plant and packing house, we had several hundred larger sheds with a single packing house. This more than doubled the earlier output per man-hour of labor, and the capital costs were much reduced. The steel was joined by electric welding, not then approved for larger structures. We also saved considerable steel by applying new engineering to the design. With these innovations I think it is safe to estimate that our costs were about half the average of our competitors.

With simple sheds and steel tables, duplicated hundreds of times in each plant, no detailed plans for new construction were necessary: we could decide on a new plant and have it built and running in four months, a turnaround in sharp contrast to our practice nowadays when it may take years to obtain the governmental permits, to get the lawyers to agree on the wording of a contract, engineers to give us exact blueprints, and the purchasing department to call in bids on needed equipment. The speed of action in those earlier days was fundamental to our success.

Competitors followed our new ideas, but they were some years behind us.

During this period of rapid expansion of the business, we lived in Weston in rented houses. As early as 1922, my rising income had inspired us to build a house of our own. We bought land in Weston, but building was postponed until 1928. By the time we decided to build, we had three children and a fourth on the way. With the help of the architect, William T. Aldrich, we developed blueprints for a beautiful stone house of more than a dozen rooms. Our thirteen acres of woods and fields, bordering on a lovely brook and two ponds, were ideal for our young family. There were pastures for our ponies, water areas for boating in summer and skating in winter, woods to roam in and streams for fishing. It was near the Meadowbrook School, reached by a path along the brook, and not far from the golf and tennis club. We named it Hidden Hearth. Above all, it was a pleasant neighborhood with congenial friends and lots of children the age of ours.

I borrowed a good deal of the money needed to finance the construction and furnishing. We moved in by September of 1929, just before the stock market crash. Then in 1930, with the advent of the Great Depression, trouble came in large doses. The prices and volume of carbon black sales fell sharply. Both the company and I were heavily in debt. Virginia's normal robust health was impaired by pneumonia, and I went through the discomfort of a case of shingles from which I was just recovering when news came from West Virginia that Jim was ill with an intestinal malady, followed by high fever and paralysis of his left side. I rushed to Charleston and brought him back to Boston where he was diagnosed to have a brain tumor. At the Peter Bent Brigham Hospital he had several unsuccessful operations. He needed a place for continuing care and I offered our summer home in Cohasset that my uncles had built for us. On a Sunday in late May, I went to get it ready and after a heavy day's work felt a sore throat coming on. By Tuesday evening it seemed much better, but in the night I woke with a high fever and was soon very sick indeed, under intensive care. Frightful pains kept me in a sleepless agony which no drugs would control. My own memory is only of a terrible pain invading my whole body, but I know that for weeks I was repeatedly in delirium, that I sometimes shouted and talked of business and financial problems, that I was taken in and out of hospitals and seen by countless doctors who talked of streptococci and general sepsis and possible localization of the infection. Weeks passed. Every hour was an agony. One day I woke from a delirium to find myself in a strange room with a large male nurse holding me in bed. I was in frightful pain. I asked for the doctor, for my wife. I tried to get up, but was forcibly detained. In despair I asked for a glass of water, and as the nurse turned away, I grabbed his chair, swung it at the window breaking out the sash and yelled into the street for the police. Other nurses came running in and put me in a straitjacket.

After a long wait, a doctor arrived who explained that I was in a mental sanitarium. Virginia was summoned and hurried to my bedside. After some discussion it was decided that she could take me home where I was put under the care of a young doctor, Henry Hamilton, who had just graduated from Harvard Medical School. I got steadily weaker. My weight went down to under ninety pounds and there were new pains in my back. There seemed little chance of recovery, but our family doctor, Fresenius Van Nuys, never lost faith. He continued to bring new specialists in for consultation. My brother, too, was weakening. He was in Cohasset and I in Weston. In early July it was decided that the great urologist, J. Dellinger Barney, would operate on me expecting to find a perinephritic abscess. At the Massachusetts General Hospital the operation was performed and they found a large, strep abscess, not next to the kidney, but below the psoas minor. When I came out of ether, I felt sure I would fully recover. The doctors were somewhat less sanguine and strongly recommended that I never resume my business responsibilities.

Within a few hours of the operation, shocking news reached me. My brother had died while I was too sick to know it. (It was later discovered, by autopsy, that he too had had a strep abscess.) Winslow Duerr, my close friend and associate, had committed suicide in the belief that his marriage was a failure. It seemed as if I would never again lead a normal or productive life.

My father, who had run unsuccessfully for mayor of Cambridge and now lived in Boston, called on my sister's husband, Ralph Bradley, to leave his cotton business and become a vice-president of the company; but much of the day-to-day responsibility of running the business during those difficult months fell on the junior executives, Ned Billings, Russ Allen, Buck Burdette, and Chandler Oakes.

I was soon out of the hospital, and after ten days of recovery at home we took our three sons, aged six, seven, and almost nine to an island in Lake Winnipesaukee. This island and the camp on it had been owned by the late Colonel Cummings, a wealthy bachelor, who had left it for members of the Wellington family to use. My mother-in-law, Mrs. Wellington, who had helped look after all four children during my illness, continued to care for the infant Linda during our absence. We stayed in New Hampshire until late September.

I had a lot of recovering to do and a new outlook on life to acquire. At first we merely rusticated, but as I grew stronger, all five of us went on long hikes in the White Mountains. It was a wonderful summer for Virginia and the boys, a paradise for me. Physical, mental, and spiritual wounds were healing and I gradually developed a less intense disposition and a greater interest in matters not related to business.

This sickness was a turning point in my career and in my family life. Whether my delirium was due to overwork and mental instability may be questioned, but of one thing I am certain: the change in life style enhanced my happiness and improved my effectiveness as a business leader.

When the boys returned for school in the fall I returned to the office, but only for a few hours a day and with a very different attitude toward the job and toward my mission in life. It was several years before I was to work full time again. Of necessity I was learning a routine that left the business detail to others. I would arrive early at the office and until the mid-1930's usually went home for lunch, and spent the afternoon at physical exercise. This rarely meant competitive sports. More often it was working around Hidden Hearth, or riding a horse on the many bridlepaths in that vicinity. I took a great interest in improving these paths and always carried a sharp hatchet on my rides. Now I had time to reflect on business strategy and policies, rather than worry about operating problems. I learned that leaving detail to others and concentrating on the decisions that really mattered made me a better chief executive for a growing company.

To broaden my outlook and vary the foci for my attention, I accepted directorships of the First National Bank of Boston, United Fruit Company, and other international business firms. These gave opportunities for travel and experience in multi-national operations. My own financial worries were assuaged by loans from my maternal uncles and gifts from my father. The company survived, and as the national economy improved, its finances gradually recovered. Under the leadership of Ned Billings, its reputation for technical preeminence advanced to new levels, sales increased, and the company resumed its growth in earnings. Then in 1937 a devastating price war hit the industry. It was entirely due to our developing a revolutionary process of pelletizing and handling carbon black.

When made in the flame, carbon black is a light flocculent powder. Like cocoa, it tends to stick to everything and won't

quickly a price war started which brought the price down below the actual out-of-pocket costs. Looking back, it is easy to say that we should have made the first bulk shipment at a reduced price, but the whole process was such an experiment that we really didn't know how much saving might accrue for either the producer or the consumer. In any case, the price remained unprofitable until after the price freeze in World War II was relaxed. The cost to the industry was enormous and precipitated a catastrophic shortage of channel black at the end of the war which resulted in the rapid development of black made by the furnace process and of a quality that soon proved superior.

This price war was a bitter blow to us, but no more so than the patent war of the same period. The invention of our pelletizing process grew from the observation that flocculent materials when stirred tend to form small spheres or pellets. Billings concluded that if these were continuously separated out, the balance of the material would go on forming spherical agglomerates. We succeeded in licensing our patents and techniques to part of the industry, but others among our competitors developed somewhat different methods to accomplish similar results. We lost suits to enforce our patents. Then after pelletizing and shipping in bulk had been well established, an old patent was discovered, owned by Binney & Smith but never exploited, which described an expensive method of making dustless pellets by mixing black with gasoline and water and decanting the liquids. Suit was brought by the owner which was defeated in the District Court, won on appeal to the Circuit Court, but lost in the U.S. Supreme Court. The Patent Commissioner later allowed a minor change in the wording of this Binney & Smith patent, and a new suit was brought. How it would have fared I cannot say because the War Production Board forced a settlement for a nominal sum by using the government's war power to renegotiate contracts. Thus, our development of pelletizing and bulk shipping only won us the privilege of paying large legal bills. But it changed the whole industry. Today, most of the world's carbon black is pelletized and shipped in bulk.

Besides leading in this development, Ned Billings was the operating head of the company's business throughout most of the 1930's. As a research chemist, in World War I he had worked under Kohler in the development of Lewisite, a dreadful mustard gas. He was very determined that in another war he would not be caught in a laboratory or an office. After Chamberlain's agreement with Hitler in Munich, he was certain war was coming. Within days he obtained a commission as a reserve line officer in the United States Navy. He was soon called to active duty on the cruiser, *U.S.S. Quincy*, patrolling the Atlantic sea lanes. In August, 1942 he was lost in the Pacific; the *Quincy* was sunk in the Battle of Savo Island while defending the landings on Guadalcanal.

With Ned's departure, it again became necessary for me to lead the day-to-day operations of the company. After Pearl Harbor the lack of rubber caused severe curtailment of tire production. We were forced to make difficult decisions with respect to personnel and plants, for there would be no need for our carbon black until the rubber plantations of the East Indies were recaptured or until new plants were established to produce a synthetic substitute.

We had always designed and built our own plants, and during the late 1920's we had as many as 4,000 workers, most of whom we had trained to cut and weld and shape steel, the very skills now most needed for building ships and war equipment. During the Depression we kept many of them busy building pumping units and other equipment needed by the oil industry. Now these men were needed for war work. Our shops and headquarters were in the Texas Panhandle, too far inland to do much shipbuilding, but we did obtain some contracts for landing craft, pontoons, and smaller items.

Munitions manufacturers are pictured as fat and greedy with

cigars in their mouths and bagfuls of dollars. We got into the munitions business in World War II not just in the hope of making a profit in a profitless year, but mainly because we had some idle engineers we didn't want to lose—and every one of us wanted to help in the war effort. We invested our own money in the electric furnace and heavy press to make large calibre cannon barrels. We didn't make a profit from our weapons business until long after the war was over. In the Korean War we received quite profitable orders for the guns we had by then learned to make at costs below any competition and which were needed in the Far East and for rearming Europe.

As we were getting into the gun business we did meet one munitions dealer who lived up to the caricature. He called the manager of our shops department in Pampa, Texas, by telephone to say that he had heard from the Army Ordnance office in St. Louis that we were looking for munitions orders and that he could get us the orders and set us up in business. Our manager, a young Texas engineer named Baker, telephoned me to say that he didn't like the odor of the conversation and he wanted my advice. He said that he asked the promoter why we should deal through him and not directly with the Army and what he expected to get for his service. The promoter told Baker that he had a friend in Army Ordnance, a retired brigadier general, who had just returned to service, and that he would like to bring this general to Pampa to explain the deal in fuller detail. I told Baker that I thought it would be better if he called the promoter back to suggest that he and the general come to Boston to discuss the deal with me.

When the promoter and his general arrived they talked about forming a company which would borrow $25,000,000 from the Army and build an addition to our shops department, and make cannon tubes by the latest process. There was a good deal of conversation about equipment and specifications, but my questions to the promoter about ownership of the new company and what he expected for himself from the deal elicited only a hazy response about his having been "Trumanized" so that he couldn't accept a participation in the ownership. But he was sure I could find some other means of compensating him. This, it developed, meant that his activities had already been questioned by the Truman Committee of the Senate and that he didn't dare accept any overt stock ownership, but required some sort of covert fee. As my questioning became more specific, the general excused himself to go to the toilet and the promoter suggested that for himself he thought I might make him a vice-president and advisor to Baker as president of the new company at a salary of $250,000 per year. As for the general, of course he couldn't accept anything except travel expenses (which he was already being provided by the promoter, including a shared apartment in St. Louis). I told the promoter I didn't see how I could accept this proposal as we were currently paying Baker only $450 per month and that my own salary was only a fraction of the figure he suggested for himself.

After my guests had left, I immediately called my friend Laurence Lombard in the legal department of the War Production Board in Washington and told him the whole story. The next day a colonel of the Judge Advocate Department of the Army arrived at my office to take a deposition. And that is the last I have heard of the promoter or the general.

In 1942 we did get an order for cannon tubes dealing directly with the St. Louis office of Army Ordnance and we built the necessary addition to our shop in Pampa, still headed by Baker at a modest increase in salary. Our contract called for forging large gun barrels of improved steel, carefully heat-treated to give the Allied artillery a punch far exceeding anything they had when the war began. The team of Texans we recruited for the plant near Pampa was the first to get into production and to meet the specifications of several new gun designs. We were proud of the awards they received for their achievements.

Shortly after Pearl Harbor, President Roosevelt appointed a committee chaired by Bernard Baruch to consider how to cope with the rubber shortage caused by Japan's conquest of Southeast Asia. When its report was published calling for the establishment of a synthetic rubber industry with a capacity to produce more than 1,100,000 long tons per year, it became apparent to us that the carbon black capacity of the country would also have to be expanded severalfold. We wrote a memo to this effect and sent it to our major customers. This was most salutary when two years later we were summoned by a Senate committee to answer charges blaming our industry for the shortage.

The fact was that there was disagreement in Washington as to what kinds of black would be needed to compound the new synthetic rubber. Most members of our industry wanted to expand but the War Production Board (WPB) delayed decision on issuing the Certificates of Necessity without which no expansion was possible. We had concluded that for many purposes the semi-reinforcing furnace black would be suitable and would extend the limited rubber supply more than would fully-reinforcing channel black.

Throughout the war we had applications pending at WPB to build such furnace black plants, and I made countless tiring trips to Washington to plead for action, often standing all night on the crowded trains. On one trip, having been unable to get an appointment to see my friend Bradley Dewey, the rubber czar for WPB, I walked into his office unannounced and found him dictating. I said without apology, as his secretary started to leave, "Brad, as sure as God made little apples, there's going to be a helluva carbon black shortage when the synthetic rubber production starts, and it is likely to frustrate your whole program." He called back the secretary and dictated a note to Donald Nelson quoting me verbatim. Nelson, a former Sears executive, headed the whole war supply program for President Roosevelt and this note appeared in the Truman Committee hearings when the shortage was under investigation at the end of the war. Fortunately, Harold Boeschenstein, a very able vice-chairman, was soon given the problem and we were allowed to start with all possible speed building several new furnace black plants.

One of these projects was stopped briefly by a frustrating order from Washington. This was signed by Charlie Eliot who had grown up a few doors from me in Cambridge. He was a grandson of Harvard's President Eliot and his family was known to Roosevelt, who had appointed him to plan for the country's postwar needs. I knew he was a distinguished landscape architect, but he was so inexperienced that I couldn't believe him competent for such a colossal task. He granted me a hearing and I rushed to Washington and persuaded him to rescind the order.

These wartime episodes are interesting today in the light of the concern of Congress for conflicts of interest between the presidential appointees and the businesses from which they come. In those days many important decisions were made by dollar-a-year men borrowed from industry and continuing to receive salaries from industry. Mostly these were patriotic volunteers who alone had the expertise needed to manage the disruptions of war. I doubt that the war could have been won without them. The Truman Committee had a very important role in finding those few who acted from self interest. If ever there is another war let us hope we can find watchdogs of like competence.

I have said that most of our new capacity in the war used the furnace process which made only semi-reinforcing black. For many years we and others had tried to make, in furnaces using both oil and gas as raw material, a carbon black that would be fully reinforcing in rubber. We were well aware that the impingement, or channel, process was extremely wasteful of gas, but no other product served as well. Long before the war, the Henry L. Doherty Laboratory of Cities Service in Toledo had successfully developed a semi-reinforcing black made from gas in a furnace. Doherty personally had acquired the patents and started commercial production in Texas near our Pampa operations. My friendship for Carl Wright, the manager of this plant, led to the knowledge that he wanted to expand but couldn't interest Doherty's widow, the sole owner of the plant, in any further investment. We arranged a bank loan and helped Wright build a second plant in Guymon, Oklahoma. It was now apparent that these two plants had insufficient capacity to meet the needs of the new synthetic rubber program. The owner of the process refused to license, so we decided to infringe. As soon as we could obtain permission from WPB, we built much larger plants of our own. At the end of the war we were able to acquire the patents by buying the earlier plants from Mrs. Doherty, thus avoiding litigation over infringement.

Early in the war Phillips Petroleum had begun making carbon black from oil by a furnace process at Borger, Texas. But the product was of a special quality without the strength suitable for tire treads. Toward the war's end a new and better Phillips product appeared on the market. This revolutionized the industry by using a process quite different as to plant, raw material, and economics from the old channel black method.

We were quick to realize the potential of this new process and set our research staff to study it intensively. Luckily we were first to discover the basic reason responsible for its success. This was the aromaticity of the raw material. Phillips had hit upon the process by accident while seeking an outlet for a light fuel oil made at Borger which happened to be aromatic. We filed a number of patent applications but assumed that most of the claims would duplicate prior claims by Phillips. As we got into commercial production, first at Ville Platte, Louisiana, where we had been making semi-reinforcing black from gas, and later in large new plants near Franklin, Louisiana, and at Big Springs, Texas, Phillips approached us about a license, asking a fee which was more than we could afford. No patents had been issued, but the patent office had notified us of interferences with respect to many of our claims. After months of negotiation, an agreement was reached under which we paid Phillips one million dollars in cash, gave them the right to use our patents when issued and obtained the right to use theirs. We also agreed to join our research in carbon black into a cooperative effort for a minimum of three years, and we appointed them agent for licensing others on the basis that they would receive eighty percent of the proceeds. Because they were the pioneers, we expected they would get the basic patents.

In essence, we bought a pig in a poke, and it took little time to discover that we didn't get much of a pig. For the most part their patent applications covered only non-essential elements of furnace design, whereas ours covered basic technology. At their insistence, the agreement was limited to North America. It later developed that our most valuable claim was not allowed in the United States but was allowed elsewhere. The agreement terminated at the end of the initial three years, and in the long run our license fees far exceeded theirs. Phillips had the honor and we the major profit from pioneering in the techniques of the present industry.

Before World War II, two of our competitors, Columbian and United, led us in tonnage of black produced by substantial margins. But after the war, as the industry rapidly shifted from channel black to furnace black, we became by far the largest producer and the only producer of all the different grades of carbon black used in rubber, plastics, paint, printing ink, and other industries.

Until the late 1930's, virtually all of the world's carbon black was made in the United States. Much of it was exported, and we had agents in the principal industrial countries to serve our overseas customers. Only in this country were there large sources of natural gas so near large tire plants as to make investment in a carbon plant attractive. After Hitler began to expand the German hegemony, we became aware that black similar to channel black was being made in Cologne from a coal tar fraction. We thought this must be a hopelessly expensive process only suitable for dire wartime needs. When Poland was invaded we advised the British of our estimates, and a very tight embargo on carbon black was established. But after the war, when Allied technicians had access to German records, we were surprised to find how economical their process was. This was due to the high yields and low cost in Germany of the anthracene residue which was the principal raw material. On learning these facts, the British decided to establish a plant in England. I flew to England to persuade the Royal Commission studying this project that the new American oil furnace black process would be better for the British economy.

I spent six weeks in London at the Savoy Hotel on the Strand. At this time the shortages of war and consequent austerities were not yet over, but by saving my ration stamps while at the hotel, I had a priceless gift for luxury-starved hostesses and managed to get invited to country houses for every weekend. Persuading the British government we had a sound proposal was not so easy, and when I returned to Boston I found it equally difficult to convince my associates and the company's directors that an investment in Britain could be profitable. The European economy was looking hopeless, but I believed that England would survive and would need carbon black. It was not until I said that I would take a license from the company and put my own money into an English plant that the opposition of my associates began to melt. After the Marshall Plan was instituted, the situation in Europe looked better, and we became the first company to negotiate with our government for a remittability guaranty which we deemed necessary to recoup our dollar investment from profits in British currency. Such guaranties under the Marshall Plan soon became the norm and were an important element in European recovery. Our negotiations took months, and it was only in 1949 that we were ready to build in England. The investment we made proved to be very profitable to us and a boon to the British economy.

It should be explained that when natural gas was the raw material for carbon black it was uneconomical to transport the gas and make the product near the markets; but with the advent of the new process, using as raw material a heavy oil that could be transported in tankers to any seaport at little cost, it became cheaper to manufacture near the larger markets. We were the first to envision a carbon black industry which would spread to all industrial countries of the world, and we became the pioneers in this development. From the end of the war, we were busy negotiating plants in most of the countries with facilities to make rubber tires.

I became very active in these negotiations and spent a great deal of time abroad. It was an exciting activity. Such negotiations are never a nine-to-five, every-weekday kind of occupation. There were many opportunities for weeks of skiing in the Alps, or motor trips in Europe, Africa, South America, or Australia. Travel and sports became so intermingled with business that I cannot separate them in this account. I will mention here only a few successes and failures which had an impact on the history of the company.

Our first overseas plant was built at Ellesmere Port, across the Mersey from Liverpool and not far from the lovely walled town of Chester. Our oldest son Louis, who was working for the company in Texas, was selected by the organization there to take charge of building this plant, and he quickly showed his leadership both in the active construction and in the negotiations with government, labor, suppliers, and customers. He had graduated from Harvard with highest honors, majoring in engineering and applied physics. Being in the Naval Reserve, he was immediately inducted into active service and sent to the California Institute of Technology for further training in aeronautical engineering, where he received the highest marks ever given. He became technical assistant to Admiral Richardson, who was in charge of fighter plane procurement, and remained in the Navy until 1946. Shortly after demobilization, he took an accelerated M.B.A. course at Harvard Business School, and upon receiving his degree went to Texas for further training in the company. His selection for the leadership of the English enterprise and his success in it led to his being returned to Boston in 1952, where he soon became treasurer of the company. Eight years later I made way for him to become president and chief executive.

Our second overseas plant was built in the south of France a few miles west of Marseilles, on the Étang de Berre. There we bought an abandoned airplane factory on the shore and used the old hangars for warehouses. The plant is not far from the delightful town of Aix and the beautiful countryside of Provence.

Our third plant was built near the historic city of Ravenna, Italy, and our visits there permitted us to renew our acquaintance with the beautiful Italian lakes, to ski in the Apennines, and to revisit Rome and the hilltowns of northern Italy.

When these new plants were inaugurated, it was our practice to invite groups of customers and government officials to see them, and it was my duty to make a speech and to try to show more familiarity with the language than I usually possessed. This was mostly good fun. At Berre, for instance, we had a special train bring us from Paris to the plant where we were met by ferry boats at the dock. With pretty girls serving champagne, we crossed the salt lake to the deep canal which connects with the Mediterranean. After returning to the plant we were served luncheon in a hangar, followed by speech making. At Ravenna we also had a special train and luncheon served in the plant, followed by a tour of the many attractions of the town, and then a large dinner at a nearby resort.

While in Milan, in connection with our Italian venture, I received a telephone call from Holland which started negotiations with friends in the Ketjen company. These led to our building a plant in Rotterdam for which we provided the technical advice and forty percent of the capital. The inauguration of this plant was one of the most gala affairs I ever attended. We were asked to bring dress suits, top hats, and formal dresses for the ladies. This was a bit of a burden in the age of airplane travel. The party was at Haarlem in the famous art museum, and we had limousines take us there from our hotel in Amsterdam. The head of the Ketjen company, Dirk de Jong, was then very much of a leading citizen. In 1940 he was only a young salesman when the Low Countries were invaded. The day of the invasion, he received a phone call from a leading Jewish merchant with whom he was barely acquainted. This man wanted to come to see de Jong at his home by way of the back door. When he came, he told de Jong that he wanted him to take over all of the Dutch properties of his firm. De Jong became one of the main elements in the underground for getting Jews out of the Netherlands. The Gestapo was never able to get information about his activities, and he survived the war to receive the eternal gratitude of the entire Jewish community. To show their gratitude, they provided us not only with this marvellous dinner party in the museum with an orchestra playing symphonic music, but also art experts to tell us about each of the famous pictures in that large collection. There must have been two hundred people at the party, including many important businessmen and statesmen, and the half dozen of us from Boston.

Another amusing inauguration took place at Cartagena, Colombia. After visiting our new plant across the bay we had a luncheon in a huge tent near the city. It was very hot with the wine flowing freely before and during lunch. My speech in Spanish, a language in which I was not fluent, was followed by responses from the mayor and governor. There were some 400 guests, and I imagine most of them realized that during these long speeches in an unfamiliar language I had fallen asleep. I was awakened by a dig in the ribs to realize that the governor had produced from under the table a large plaque cast in metal which he was presenting to me for the entrance gate to the plant. I have never been very good at extemporaneous remarks, and when I staggered to my feet amid the guffaws, all I could think of was to say, "muchas gracias."

One day while skiing at Klosters, Switzerland, in 1955, I received a telephone call from Boston saying a cable from Melbourne had been received advising that a vice-president of United Carbon was in Australia and had announced to the leading customers that they would build a plant at Geelong in partnership with Shell. This was a blow because our British plant had captured more than two-thirds of the Australian market. I telephoned John Andrews, the head of our Paris office, and we rushed to Melbourne. We soon learned that United's man had been in Australia for six weeks negotiating for raw material, a plant site, and permits from the Australian government. It looked as if we were too late, but our calls on the four tire manufacturers in that country told us that, although United had been given considerable encouragement from that quarter, there was not yet a real commitment because United had not been willing to promise a price unprotected by import duty. After a week's negotiation we were able to get a tentative commitment from these four customers that if we built a plant and guaranteed the world price net of tariff we would be in a position to keep sixty percent of the business. In the meantime, we were testing raw material from the two refineries, Stanvac and Shell, and found the former preferable. We announced in the press that we would build a plant in Altona. On our return to Boston, Shell sent representatives from London to see us, protesting that they would be forced to retaliate against such an unfriendly act. We were prepared for the protest with comparative costs and were able to convince them that we could hardly have done otherwise. Shell decided to withdraw.

All of these plants have now been very much enlarged from their original capacity; the markets have continued to grow, and

Early carbon black plant of G. L. Cabot at Cabot, Pennsylvania.

Drilling for gas in Calhoun County, West Virginia, about 1900.

Shipping carbon black at Grantsville, West Virginia, in 1905.

Our first channel black plant in Texas was at Eliasville and started operation early in 1926. It was located in an oil field where the casinghead gas produced with the oil had been wasting into the air. It was highly profitable from the start. We built nine such plants with our own construction crews in the five years before the Great Depression.

The channel black plants we built were remote from towns and we had to build houses for the workers. We tried to improve the quality of life with trees and gardens, club houses, and playing fields, especially in the sand hills of West Texas.

A channel black plant consists of thousands of small gas flames impinging on steel channels from which the soot is scraped to fall into hoppers as the channels move back and forth a few feet.

The hot houses of a channel black plant are of sheet iron on a light iron frame. Each contains a table, the iron channels forming the top. The many duplicate sections make it possible to build a plant from crude sketches used to buy a bill of material, and with a large work force spread over a wide area construction can be rapid. Here is a table being erected.

A large channel black plant in the Texas Panhandle.

Hidden Hearth, our home in Weston since 1929.

Our three sons, Louis, Tommie and Rob born in 1921, 1922 and 1924, were followed by a daughter Linda in 1928. This 1930 photo does not include a fourth son Ned born in 1943.

Hiking in the White Mountains of New Hampshire with my three sons in search of a new life style after my severe illness of 1930.

Ned Billings at the wheel of *Ave-linda*. It was he who held the Company together during the early 1930's. He was killed in the Battle of Savo Island protecting the landings on Guadalcanal. Our surgeon son, born the following year, was named for him.

The first car to carry carbon black successfully in bulk. I designed it in 1932. The bulk handling of pelletized black revolutionized the industry.

A gasoline plant extracting liquids from casinghead gas in the Texas oil fields.

Forging gun barrels at Pampa, Texas. An operation started in
World War II and still continued.

A modern furnace black plant on the Intra-Coastal Canal near Franklin,
Louisiana, built and operated by Cabot Corporation.

The first furnace black plant in Europe. The Stanlow Plant of Cabot Carbon, Ltd. on the Mersey in Cheshire near Liverpool. This was the first unit. The present plant at this site has been enlarged ten fold.

Speaking in Italian at the opening of our Ravenna plant.

Cabot's French furnace black plant on the Étang de Berre.

Awarded the medal of the Legion of Honor by Jean Savelli, Consul-General of France.

Virginia in the Superstition
Mountains of Arizona riding
among the saguaro, cholla,
greasewood and ocotillo plants.

Teaching the family to navigate on *Avelinda*, 1937.

A beggar on horseback.

competing plants have been built. But by being first in the field, we have held on to the largest share. Although we were the first to build in a majority of those countries which made substantial quantities of rubber tires, our efforts haven't always been entirely successful.

There were a number of industrial countries where we failed and our competitors were the first to establish new carbon black plants. In Mexico, Phillips succeeded in negotiating with the government where we had failed. In India, we reached an agreement with an Indian industrialist to build a jointly-owned plant which would have been a great boon to that country, but after spending many thousands of dollars, unforeseen burdens imposed by the government caused us to withdraw. Much more favorable concessions were later granted to two of our American competitors. In Brazil we thought we had made a deal to build a plant only to find that we were misled. Now, twenty years later, we have a joint venture there. In South Africa, we tried building a plant in partnership with local capitalists, but after I had spent some weeks selecting a plant site, arranging for raw materials, and negotiating with the local government, the national government decided to make its own investment in partnership with Phillips and went ahead to build a plant on the very site I had selected.

From a personal standpoint, these failures were not a total loss, for in each case my wife and I were able to enjoy pleasant visits to those parts of the world while I was engaged in negotiations. There were also other countries where we enjoyed visits to study the economics of carbon black production but decided against establishing plants.

CHAPTER VI

❧

Diversification

IN the early days, carbon black plants were established where there was no market for the gas discovered while drilling for oil. It was cheap to buy the gas or the wells themselves when only gas was found. But as supplies from these wells declined, we began to do the drilling ourselves. Thus the drilling of exploratory wells became the earliest diversification in our business. Until the 1930's, however, drilling was confined to West Virginia and to the proximity of our existing gas lines. After the Depression we began to acquire some gas leases in the Panhandle areas of Oklahoma and Texas. By the end of the decade it became apparent that there were very important gas reserves under these leases, and we made a contract with the eastern gas companies associated with Standard Oil to become the principal supplier to a very large gas line projected from these leases to the markets in the Pittsburgh–Cleveland areas. It was necessary to get permission from the Federal Power Commission (FPC) to build this line, and a small truckload of exhibits was prepared to present to the hearing. The evening before the scheduled hearing, the FPC granted to Curtis Dall, President Roosevelt's son-in-law, a permit to supply similar eastern markets from south Texas based on little more than a letter from the White House. Standard Oil felt obliged to withdraw its project. Within a week, Dall arranged to sell his permit for $900,000 to Wagner and Symonds of Chicago Corporation, who, with the help of New York friends, managed to finance the pipeline. This was the start of the multi-billion dollar Tenneco. We then contracted to supply from these leases the gas needed for a proposed pipeline to the Chicago–Milwaukee area. When this project also fell through, we were left in the middle of World War II with no market and, therefore, no ability to get the pipe needed to develop the leases, which would expire unless exploited. This left us no choice but to sell our leases at a small fraction of the true value to a company that had a pipe-line contract. However, our success in finding large reserves stimulated us to do other exploration, and a modest success in drilling for oil and gas has continued to the present.

We also found success in the natural gasoline business. We sold our plant at Salem, West Virginia, to Standard Oil, but we built other gasoline plants in Texas and other western states. These produced the liquid petroleum gases (LPG) butane and propane, along with the heavier liquids marketed as natural gasoline. When these plants were established, there was practically no market for LPG.

In 1955 we were asked to participate in a Texas plant to make butadiene and aviation gasoline from butane, which was of interest to us because of our difficulty in marketing our output of the raw material. Because butadiene is the main component of most synthetic rubbers, we naturally discussed this proposal with our major customers among the tire manufacturers. While a company was being formed, the leading participant suddenly withdrew and we thought the project was defunct. But those customers who needed the product urged us not to abandon the idea. We had to take over the negotiation from the promoter and succeeded in forming jointly with Loeb, Rhodes & Company of New York a company called Texas Butadiene & Chemical (TB&C) to build, largely with loan money, a plant near Houston. The plant was in operation only a short time when a minor economic recession and oversupply of butadiene greatly curtailed its operations. The company was in danger of default on its bank loans, and in the winter of 1957–58, while my wife and I were in Europe, we received a telephone call asking me to go to Akron to seek help. My mission there was unsuccessful. On the night flight back to rejoin my wife in Paris, I felt quite dejected about the prospect of not being able to avoid bankruptcy. Brooding over this, it occurred to me that we might just be able to establish an outlet for butadiene in France by using its exchange controls remaining from the era of European dollar shortages to our advantage. I made a call on the ministry for industry suggesting that if we were given an import permit for two years' supply of synthetic rubber needed by the French tire industry, we would undertake to invest twenty-five percent of the proceeds in a synthetic rubber plant in France and later undertake to establish a French butadiene industry. Of course, we didn't have any synthetic rubber, but I felt confident we could barter butadiene for rubber, since there was a surplus capacity worldwide for making rubber copolymers from butadiene. The ministry received my idea cordially enough, although I won't burden this story with the countless obstacles we encountered in other ministries. Suffice it to say that after some months of negotiation we had a deal under which a French company, Société d'Elastomers Synthèse (SES), was formed and in which TB&C owned a thirty-seven percent interest, the remainder being owned by Shell, Michelin, and other French industrial companies. The outlet for butadiene provided by the barter arrangement saved our Texas enterprise. The French company was ultimately sold to Shell, and the Texas company to Sinclair, in each case at a handsome profit, and we have been closely associated with Loeb, Rhodes & Company ever since.

During the more critical years of SES, it was part of my job to attend monthly directors' meetings in Paris. Except in the summer or when in Europe on other business, this ordinarily took me only twenty-four hours Boston to Boston. It wasn't much of an ordeal, for I would leave on the jet flight in the early evening, fly economy class where I nearly always had three seats in a row and wasn't kept awake by the proffered wines and many-course first-class dinner. On arrival in Paris at 8:00 A.M. (2:00 A.M. Boston time), I would be taken by limousine to the Shell office and there would confer with the French chairman to decide what seemed to be in the best interest of the French and American investors. At 11:00 A.M., the directors representing other French investors would arrive, and we would proceed to get their concurrence with our plans. While lawyers drafted votes, we would wine and dine in lavish French fashion, and at 3:00 P.M., the directors representing two labor unions would appear. At this point the conversation, which was in English up to now, would switch to French. Through this I would doze, to be awakened by my chauffeur who would take me to Orly airport whence I flew somewhat comatose back to Boston, arriving in time to have a pleasant evening with my wife before retiring and making up any lost sleep. Next morning I would feel completely refreshed.

As a result of my having established the first carbon black plant and the first successful synthetic rubber plants in France and the first carbon black plant in Italy, I have been given honorary awards by both those countries.

Much of the final negotiation with respect to the French project was handled by our son Tom, who was then living in France. His performance so impressed our New York friends that he was hired to promote similar projects in other countries. He later became president of TB&C, International. His office was in Lausanne, his residence in Geneva, and his secretary in New York, but he lived mostly in an airplane. The largest venture on which he and I worked was the attempt to establish in southern Argentina a huge petrochemical complex to include a carbon black plant and a synthetic rubber plant. The Frondisi government wanted this located inland on the Deseado River in windswept Patagonia, but after I visited the site, we persuaded them to let us move it to the coast at Puerto Deseado. The project was all set to go with a major portion of the financing provided by European equipment credits. The senior thirteen million dollars was to have been from the Ex-Im Bank in Washington, with a closing on Friday. Earlier in the week word came that it might be postponed and we soon discovered that my friend, Jack McCloy, then chairman of the Chase Bank, had intervened, pointing out that the Ex-Im charter forbade loans where private capital was available, and that Continental Oil was prepared to build a plant in Argentina. The delay caused the elaborate financial plans for our project to collapse like a house of cards. Naturally, I was distressed at the time but have since thanked McCloy for his intervention. The competing project didn't get going for another five years and proved a disaster for the American companies investing in the venture.

In addition to our venture in the butadiene business, we made a number of other diversification attempts. Mention was made of our making equipment for the oil industry and our entry into the gun business. Those shops, near Pampa, Texas, were now enlarged to make various items of machinery, especially well-servicing equipment and large, mobile drilling rigs. In connection with licensing the Germans to make oil furnace black, we acquired a license to make a silica fume used as a thickening or thixotropic agent. This is now produced in an integrated plant at Tuscola, Illinois, and sold throughout the industrial world. Shortly before my retirement, we started on two ventures in the chemical industry. A pilot plant in France, to make titania, jointly owned with a French producer, led us to think that we had a viable new process for large-scale manufacture of this important white pigment. We built a multi-million dollar titania plant at Ashtabula, Ohio, which unfortunately began production during a period of distressed markets. After several years of unprofitable operation, this was sold to New Jersey Zinc who have made it a profitable investment. At the same time, we developed in our laboratory a new method of polymerizing olefins which we thought would produce a better plastic at reduced cost. This became ready for commercial use at a time when the market for polyethylene was also distressed. Negotiations to get into the plastic industry came to naught, and advancing technology finally convinced us that we would best abandon further work on our new process. We also abandoned an expensive development program for cross-linking polyethylene admixed with a special carbon black. In this case it was a poor patent position which discouraged us.

My father had dreamt of liquefying components of natural gas, and had built a small plant at Elizabeth, West Virginia, as early as 1913. The business proved unprofitable because he had no fractionating column and couldn't economically separate from the gas those hydrocarbons which can be kept liquid under pressure. This was some years before natural gasoline, extracted from natural gas, led to the present liquid petroleum gas industry and long before the development of the cryogenic process for liquefying natural gas itself, now sold as LNG. However, the experience provoked thought and in 1920 I wrote a short paper on the possibility of augmenting gas supplies during peak load periods by liquefying and storing the surplus during summer months. It was only a rough estimate of probable cost based on little reliable data. My concept was a steel tank of 55,000 barrels capacity buried in sawdust in an "ice house." After gaining the confidence of Howell Cooper of Standard Oil, I showed him this paper. He pointed out difficulties that hadn't occurred to me, such as the accumulation of ice in the sawdust which would impair its insulating value, and the brittleness of ordinary steel under such low temperatures.

Many years later the idea of transporting liquid natural gas was pioneered by an inventor named Morrison and the present LNG industry was started. We joined with other investors in studying the prospect of supplying the markets of England, France, and the United States. We participated in a minor way with a

French company in establishing imports of LNG from Algeria to France. This led to a venture to import from Algeria to New England. After months of hearings we were given a license by the FPC to import a supply of LNG to the Boston area. The order specifically stated that the FPC had no jurisdiction over the construction and use of the facilities.

Terminal facilities were built near Boston and put into operation by a wholly-owned subsidiary. In the meantime, the gas distributors in the New York area were interested in much larger imports and persuaded us, by offering a large non-recourse loan, to build another terminal on Staten Island. We contracted with the Algerians for the quantities needed, with a nullification clause if FPC approval were not obtained by December 31, 1973. On May 25th of that year, without any warning whatsoever, we got notice from the FPC that it reversed its decision on jurisdiction and required discontinuance of construction or use of any terminal facilities until new hearings. It was apparent what had happened; the original decision had been three-to-two and two of the three in the majority had retired and not yet been replaced. We couldn't comply, and had to seek a stay of sentence in the courts. This was granted and after some months the courts decided that a commission could change its mind, but only after hearings. By that time the contracts in Algiers had voided and the Arab oil embargo had caused a tripling of fuel prices. The cost of maintaining these idled facilities was more than we could bear. We had to let the Staten Island facility go to the creditor-distributor, abandoning an investment which cost us thirty-five million dollars and the gas consumers many, many times more than this.

Shortly before my retirement, the rapid expansion of the business made it necessary to lease in Boston more office space than was available at any one location, and we agreed with Travellers Insurance to lease sufficient floors to justify an investment in a new building. The high taxes in Boston had inhibited the construction of any general-purpose office building for more than twenty-five years. It was our courage in signing a twenty-year escalating lease that broke the logjam.

Other efforts at diversification since my retirement have been successful, notably the purchase of the Stellite division from Union Carbide which made us the largest producer of high performance non-ferrous alloys, and more recently the purchase of the Kawecki Company, which makes us the principal producer of specialty metals.

The business which employed only a few men when I came into the management has now grown into a great multi-national corporation employing ten thousand men and women. Its shares are held by thousands of stockholders who receive regular dividends. The growth has come from profits on the sale of products needed wherever there were people living above the level of mere subsistence.

Perhaps, if I hadn't needed a job in order to marry, I might have become a doctor, or lawyer, or teacher, or even an artist. But business is an exciting calling and I would think that business leaders are no more impelled by greed than are men and women in other professions.

Since my retirement, I have tried to use my business experience to promote desirable social change by personally investing time and money, often using the profit motive to get results. Such social engineering is a real challenge and has kept me active. When not traveling, I am in the office four days a week participating in many philanthropic ventures.

CHAPTER VII

❦

United Fruit Company

ONE part of my business career which I consider a failure was the culmination of my association with one of Boston's greatest enterprises, the banana company founded by Andrew Preston which owned thousands of acres of farms and the "Great White Fleet" of refrigerator ships.

In 1936, a year after my election to the board of The First National Bank of Boston, I was asked to join the board of United Fruit Company in which the bank's trust department had a substantial interest. I visited all of the tropical divisions and was made a member of the executive committee. The company was dominated by its president, Samuel Zemurray, who had built Cuyamel Fruit Company and merged it into United Fruit in 1929. I admired his shrewd management, and especially his devotion to the health and agricultural productivity of the people of tropical America. I became an influential member of the board because of my frequent visits to the tropics, my knowledge of Latin America, and understanding of the economics of tropical agriculture.

During World War II our ships were taken over by the War Shipping Administration and used for supplying the expeditionary forces. By war's end, our ships were returned and we were back in the banana business. Various problems arose in our relations with some of the governments of Latin America, and Zemurray felt all of them could readily be solved by a word from the Department of State. I tried to persuade him that our government's policy with respect to the Latin countries had been changed by the war, and especially by the formation of the United Nations and the Organization of American States. I felt sure my advice was well grounded, for my relations with State were closer than his, but he was not the kind of man who took advice kindly. He was paying over half-a-million dollars per year in retainers to such influential Washingtonians as Bob Lafollette, Tom Corcoran, Spruille Braden, Leon Henderson, and Edward Bernays, and I tried my best to persuade him that this was counterproductive, at best a waste of money. The argument led John Toulmin, another member of the executive committee, to ask him when he expected to retire and turn the presidency over to the executive vice-president. All of us on the committee were upset to find that he had no such plans. After months, with various committee members continually needling him, he suggested that I become president. At first I declined on the ground that I didn't know the banana business, but during my hospitalization as a result of a skiing accident, I reconsidered and finally accepted his offer knowing that Cabot Corporation had sufficient depth of management to do well without my constant attention. Zemurray announced that I would be elected president at the next annual meeting and that he would become chairman of the executive committee. I thought that our differences would disappear, but as I began to assume leadership they became exacerbated. Very soon after my election we both came to the conclusion that the arrangement wouldn't work and that we must find someone within the company to take over the presidency. He suggested Kenneth Redmond, and I concurred, with the understanding that he would let Redmond run the company. As I didn't want to hurt the company by appearing to have lost confidence in its future, I remained as director for another year. But I sold my stock and have not had further connection with the company's affairs.

Redmond had grown up in the sales department where the prevailing opinion was that Ecuadorian bananas, which had to be harvested before they were fully developed because of the longer voyage to North American markets, could never successfully compete with bananas grown in Central America. He failed to heed the advice of scientists who predicted that the airborne Sigatoka disease, which had doubled the cost of growing Central American bananas, would be delayed by the Andes and not reach Ecuadorian farms for another ten years.

Although in 1948 I had tendered my resignation, Virginia and I thought it would be interesting to motor from Bogotá to Quito over the newly completed Panamerican Highway. It was an arduous trip and we arrived in Quito hot, tired, and thirsty late in the afternoon of the fourth day to find a message asking me to come at once to the presidential palace. We thought the summons boded ill. Without stopping I left for the palace with an interpreter. When I was ushered into a large room, a big man rose, greeted me cordially in perfect English with a New York accent, apologized that he had given me no time to rest from my trip. This was Galo Plaza, who later became my good friend and co-trustee of the agriculture school of Zamorano, Honduras. He said that he was about to meet with his cabinet to consider a large loan program for banana planters and needed my advice as to how soon the advancing Sigatoka disease would reach Ecuador. I gave him the estimate of our scientists and with this assurance the loan program was approved. The export of bananas from Ecuador grew from half a million stems to more than forty-six million stems per year. Redmond left most of this for competitors to handle and the earnings of United Fruit slumped disastrously. Ecuador prospered and Plaza became a great world figure as President of the Organization of American States and a mediator of disputes in Europe and Asia.

We returned to Quito thirty years later on a trip to the Galapagos Islands and spent a weekend with the Plaza family at their lovely country place Zuleta. Here Galo has now retired to live on and manage the ancestral farm. He owns 4,000 acres of very fertile land in this broad mountain valley. Although close to the equator, it is 9,500 feet high with crops similar to a farm in England or Wisconsin. They grow wheat, barley, alfalfa, and temperate-zone fruit. They have a large herd of Holstein cows and there are two dairies and a cheese factory on the property. Poor roads and distance to town make it uneconomic to sell milk except as cheese and butter. We were delighted with our tour of the farm and its villages of smiling peasants in colorful native costume. Most beautiful is the main house, built around a paved court with stone columns and stone-faced verandas. It was built by Jesuits between 1610 and 1690 and was restored by Galo's grandfather and father. The region is noted for its wood carving and the interiors are as rich as the choir of an old cathedral, with a patina that comes from centuries of care. The hospitality of this charming family will be a fond memory forever. Especially refreshing were the views of world affairs voiced by this great man and his well-trained children.

During my active business years, I was elected president of the Commercial Club of Boston which held eight dinner meetings a year at which some prominent person was invited to speak on current problems of interest to businessmen. The club was the first of several similar commercial clubs in the United States, and during my tenure, I was asked to speak at dinners of the Chicago and the Cincinnati Clubs. I was impressed that those clubs included in their membership the chief executive officer of all the leading commercial and industrial companies in their respective cities. At a meeting of the executive committee of our club, I suggested that we discontinue the waiting list of applicants, which included mostly salesmen ambitious to sell themselves to a top notch list of potential clients, and make a concerted effort to recruit all of Boston's business leaders who were not already in the club. We were moderately successful except that the Algonquin Club, in whose clubhouse we held our dinners, refused to let us include Jews. My term as president expired before I was able to negotiate a solution to this ban, but I am happy to say that our son Louis, who became president some years later, did succeed in negotiating a settlement, and today some of the ablest and most attractive members of the Commercial Club are leading Jewish businessmen.

My presidency of United Fruit was no success but I learned from it a lesson about loyalty. If Zemurray had let me run the business without his interference, perhaps the company could have prospered. I often wonder about this. It would have taken courage as well as wisdom to meet the new conditions. I can only hope that I would have met these challenges to the banana business as I did the changes in the economics of carbon black. Without the support of Zemurray, it would have been impossible.

I have had, during my career and outside directorships, many opportunities to observe a variety of styles of organizing and running a business. My father thought of organization as a master and servant relationship, but his was a small business in which he personally could handle the smallest detail. Sam Zemurray ran the United Fruit Company like a fiefdom and did little to develop junior executives or plan for the future succession. On the other hand, I felt it important to develop decisiveness in subordinates. It was my policy to have the point of decision at the lowest level in the company that the relevant facts could be collected through normal channels. If it became my place to decide, I liked to collect the facts and opinions by dialog with associates one at a time rather than by group discussion. Son Louis prefers a committee organization for decisions, and feels that this gives the junior members a greater feeling of participation. I think most studies of this subject agree with Louis. Whichever pattern is preferred, the most important thing is not to destroy morale by second guessing after the decision has been made. An executive (and a turtle) can't make progress without exposing his neck, and won't try if he fears for it. Fear of the boss's displeasure can destroy both loyalty and initiative.

CHAPTER VIII

Government Service

MY first introduction to serving in government was as chairman of a commission for the town of Weston seeking a new water supply. With the help of a Harvard geologist, we were eminently successful and our discovery saved the town many thousands of dollars before population growth compelled it to join the metropolitan water system.

Later, my lifetime friend, Governor Leverett Saltonstall, appointed me chairman of the Massachusetts Aeronautical Commission. Then, in 1944, he asked me to be chairman of a commission to prepare plans for Logan Airport, which was to be built on the mudflats to the east of Boston Harbor. He wanted the plans to be ready for the unemployment crisis expected after demobilization. These assignments led to a number of interesting experiences. The real planning was done by the professional staff, notably Arthur Tully, Director of Aeronautics, Harry Shepley, the architect, and Miles Clair, engineer. To have their plans accepted I needed the support of other members of the commission, the Department of Public Works and, of course, that of the governor and the legislature. It was a major collaboration, and it worked.

During World War II, in addition to these duties for the Commonwealth, I was too involved in holding Cabot Corporation together to do much in Washington except as a member of various business committees created by the War Production Board.

A much greater adventure in government service came during the Korean War. At the time of my retirement from United Fruit Company I was looking for some federal government appointment to provide a more plausible explanation than "personal reasons" for resigning. Louis Johnson, the Secretary of Defense, whom I had known in West Virginia, suggested an assistant secretaryship in the Pentagon. When I told him I thought this particular job was not quite in my field, he asked whether I would be interested in the chairmanship of the Atomic Energy Commission. I was, and he asked me to meet President Truman. Secretary Johnson took me to the White House, and I'm sure that I did not leave a very good impression of myself. I found the interview embarrassingly short; I didn't get the job. I doubted the President would even remember me if my name were suggested again, as it was in the following year.

Some months after this call to the White House a group of my Boston friends invited me to a discussion of how to avoid an escalation of the Korean War. This was at that war's darkest moment. Hordes of Chinese troops had unexpectedly crossed the Yalu River and driven back the U.N. Army, under General MacArthur, all the way to Pusan. There were about forty of us Bostonians who met in Dover at the homes of Harry Cabot and Lloyd Brace. We were subsequently called by our opponents "The Dover Group." Members of the John Birch Society and other ardent anti-communist organizations even charged us with being "fellow travelers." We did publish a resolution suggesting that the U.S. position at the U.N. Assembly might show a willingness to negotiate a settlement to avert the danger of a nuclear war. But any charge that the group had communist leanings made little sense. However, the FBI did show some interest and made many inquiries about our discussion. I imagine membership in the group may have delayed security clearance for several who later served the country in sensitive positions.

Soon thereafter, I received a call from Jim Webb, then Undersecretary of State. He asked me to come to Washington to meet

Secretary of State Dean Acheson. When I arrived, Jim had assembled in his office, to persuade me that I was needed, not Acheson, but my friends Averell Harriman, Bob Lovett, and Bill Foster. I was eventually given the position of Director of International Security Affairs, to "speak for the Department of State on matters relating to the North Atlantic Treaty, other similar international programs, and military and economic assistance for mutual defense." It was a new position, working very closely with Acheson, and chairing an inter-departmental, five-man committee to allocate aid to our Allies. We were shipping enormous quantities of weapons and war material necessary for the defense of Europe and other pressure points on the periphery of the Communist world. It was important to coordinate these shipments with continuing economic aid and to stimulate our Allies' own efforts to recruit troops and increase military budgets.

I was a Republican recruited to work in a Democratic administration probably in the hope that a businessman from the opposite party would be an indication to the Congress that money wasn't being wasted. I arrived full of criticism and left full of admiration. I had ample opportunity to see how foreign policy decisions were made, for nearly everything of importance considered in the State Department impinged on my responsibilities. Rarely did domestic politics appear to be a consideration.

The organizational problems of governmental decision-making were far greater than anything I had encountered in business, but I had a high respect for the public servants with whom I worked, especially for the senior career diplomats and the military men. I developed a high regard, too, for the leaders of the Truman administration. Each morning I attended staff meetings with Acheson and his principal aides and often went to the Pentagon to confer with Marshall, Lovett or the Joint Chiefs of Staff. When there were important foreign visitors, I usually participated in the discussions.

My contacts with the President were not as frequent. When

I did see him he seemed relaxed and never the waspish man he is now pictured. I remember coming to the Oval Room at 11:00 one busy morning to get his support for a plan to move the headquarters of NATO from London to Paris. He was at his desk reading a book when I entered. After my brief explanation he asked if Acheson and Marshall concurred. Receiving my affirmative reply, he nodded assent, then asked if I had read the book he was holding. It was Dobie's history of the Texas Panhandle. When he found I knew that area, he kept me talking about it for twenty minutes.

My first experience in diplomacy came only three weeks after my arrival. We were rushing about a quarter-billion dollars worth of arms to the French army in Vietnam who were beleaguered by the forces of Ho Chi-Minh supported by Russia and China. Pleven, then Premier of France, came to Washington to ask for additional aid. With him came a number of high officials of the French government. I was invited to attend his conference with Truman as a member of the American team and sat near the President, whom we had briefed the previous day. Naturally many of the questions asked by Pleven concerned specific military equipment which they needed and these questions were referred to me. I fear my answers seemed a bit blunt to the more experienced aides, but they seemed to satisfy the President. Not since school days had I felt such stage fright. Later, when premiers from Paris, London, The Hague, and Brussels came to see Truman, I was more relaxed and enjoyed the discussions of political, military, and economic problems. These missions headed by Clement Attlee of the United Kingdom, Rene Mayer of France, Richard Stickker of the Netherlands, and Paul Spaak of Belgium included others whom I came to know better. Unfortunately, I kept no journal, nor have I preserved my correspondence of the period, and most of my acquaintanceship with the statesmen of our allies has been forgotten.

I had not known Acheson or Marshall before coming to work

with them. They were both very considerate of my inexperience and I came to have a great affection for them. When I was hard pressed in dealing with congressional committees, they gave kindly advice and never complained of my failings. Only once did I see either of them show any loss of temper and that was when Acheson spoke sharply of the secretariat to McWilliams for not keeping me informed. Actually, he was not really to blame. The incident illustrates the difficulty of coordinating action in an organization as large as government. On a Saturday about noon, I had an urgent phone call saying that Secretary Marshall was sending me an important document requiring my signature before I left for the weekend and that it was top secret and couldn't be discussed on the phone. A full colonel brought the document in a great hurry. It asked my authorization for sending $10 million to Romulo in Manila for an army payroll to be charged to my aid budget. Having been warned to suspect urgent requests on Saturday, I told the colonel I wanted to study the matter, but he refused to leave the paper with me and left in a huff. I tried to reach Dean Rusk who was the Assistant Secretary of State for the Far East, but found he had been taken to the hospital for a kidney stone emergency. Knowing there was a cabinet meeting at 10:00 A.M. on Monday, I mentioned the matter to Acheson at his staff meeting that morning. Not until then did I learn that the request from General Romulo had come directed to his good friend Secretary Marshall who had discussed it with Rusk and Acheson. Rusk was supposed to clear the matter with me, but thinking the money would come from a more secret budget, he had failed to do so. I promptly sent Marshall my apology which was gracefully accepted.

On my first meeting with Marshall, he had charmed me with kind stories about our many mutual friends in Boston. In later, more serious meetings, I was impressed with the low-keyed persuasiveness of his arguments. There was no man in Washington who was more highly respected by Congress. Acheson was very kind and patient with his staff and being trained as a lawyer, he could muster the most compelling arguments to support his views; but many in the Congress resented him, perhaps because his careful manners, perfection of diction, and impeccable dress made people think him a snob. Actually, considering his social position and his education at Groton, Yale, and Harvard, he was remarkably free from snobbery and had instinctive generosity toward those less well endowed.

I made several trips to Europe and was a delegate to the NATO meeting in Ottawa. I had close associations with our ambassadors to the European Allies and presided at a meeting of these ambassadors in London, held in the unfurnished house in Regents Park soon to become the ambassador's residence. It was at this meeting that Bob Murphy gave me the name "Simon Legree." Bob was ambassador to Belgium and thought I had been pressing too hard to get the Belgians to increase their military budget and lengthen the period of conscription. He had persuaded General Eisenhower of this and got him to write me a letter. However, it was Dave Bruce, then ambassador to France, who came to my aid and most of the heads of missions seemed to feel that the Europeans could do more to help themselves avoid further Communist aggression. Nevertheless, we never succeded in raising as much as half of the troop force which the NATO staff had said would be needed to defend Europe with conventional weapons.

These European trips usually included a visit to General Eisenhower who was then in Paris organizing the military defense of the NATO countries, and sometimes to Jack McCloy in Frankfurt who was commissioner to Germany. I naturally developed a closer understanding with my American colleagues who were helping strengthen our allies in the free world, old friends and new like Averell Harriman, Bob Lovett, Milton Katz, Lincoln Gordon, Phil Jessup, George Perkins, and many others.

In trying to persuade congressional committees of the validity of our programs, I was not always as successful as I would have hoped. As a Republican working for a Democratic administration, my contacts on Capitol Hill were often strained. But I was very fortunate in persuading Charlie Coolidge, a leader of the Boston Bar, to come to Washington as my deputy. He served brilliantly, first in the State Department and later in the Department of Defense, and in both he was loved and admired by associates. I was also fortunate in having as my closest contact in Europe, Chuck Spofford, a leading New York lawyer, who was then serving as ambassador to NATO.

Congress was evidently not altogether impressed with the results of my efforts in promoting mutual security. After I had been in Washington about a year, the new Mutual Security Act eliminated my position and transferred the duties from the Department of State to an independent agency under Harriman. Acheson very kindly offered me another assignment, but I decided to return home to Boston. I had resigned all of my business connections, but they were soon restored.

It was patriotism that had brought me to Washington at the darkest hour. I have no regrets. What I learned about our government was fair payment for my time. I worked long hours and was tired when I left. I can't say that the experience was any direct help in my business career, but it did enhance my appreciation of the problems of government and my enjoyment of keeping in touch with world affairs.

Some months after leaving Washington, I received a call from Jack Bingham who had the responsibility for the "Point Four" type of aid in the State Department. He had been a close associate of mine while I was in government, and he asked me to take a group of engineers and economists to Egypt to help the new government there with problems of industrialization. I was appointed to the job by President Truman, but returned after Eisenhower's inauguration to report to Secretary Dulles. He declined to see me, and I shortly discovered that I had lost my security clearance at State. No reason was given and I soon discovered that the file was unavailable to anyone but Assistant Secretary Scott MacLeod and (presumably) Secretary Dulles. Friends in the security division suggested that I ask for a field investigation, and when I returned to Boston an investigator called. From his questioning I realized that the reason pertained to my father's activities. When my father was past ninety, he had written a letter to the *Boston Herald*, the essence being that we should call our competitors in the cold war Stalinists rather than Communists because Jesus Christ was a Communist. As grounds for denying me service to my country, this made no sense. I sent the investigator packing and I called Jim Killian of M.I.T., asking for his advice. With his intervention and influence, to my delight, I soon received word that my clearance at State was restored through the White House. In fairness to Dulles and Eisenhower, I would like to point out that this was at the height of Senator Joe McCarthy's witch hunt. But Dulles continued his refusal to see me and heed my advice.

I had many conversations with Naguib, who was the nominal Egyptian leader, and several with Nasser and Sadat, who actually led the revolution against the corrupt Farouk government. In these talks, it was apparent that what they wanted from the United States was more than help in industrialization. They wanted arms, a steel mill, and help with the Aswan Dam. It seemed unlikely we would want to give them arms because at the time they were squabbling with the British over the size of the forces guarding the Suez Canal and over the condominium of the Sudan. My superficial study of the steel mill problem led me to believe that it would cost roughly twice as much to produce steel in Egypt as to buy it in Europe, and that it would be far better for their economy to try to develop their own labor-intensive industries less dependent on expensive raw materials. As for the Aswan Dam, I felt we could forge a strong bond of friendship with the new government by providing the foreign currency component estimated at somewhat over one hundred million dollars, and that this would help obviate Egypt's major problem of having too large a population for its food supply. I discussed these problems with my friend Hank Byroade, then serving as Assistant Secretary of Middle Eastern Affairs, and with his deputy, John Jernegan. They concurred with my analysis and encouraged me to publish my views in a number of newspaper articles. I also discussed these problems with various other friends in the Eisenhower Administration, with several members of Congress, and with Eugene Black, then president of the World Bank. Black told me that it was the policy of the bank not to make loans without the endorsement of the legislative branch of a *de jure* government, and that the revolutionary government of Egypt would hardly qualify. It is interesting to note that thirty-odd months later, under pressure from Dulles, the bank did propose a loan for the Aswan Dam. Had the proposal come earlier, it seems clear that Egypt's purchase of Soviet arms could have been avoided and the Suez crisis resulting from the withdrawal of this proposal of help with the dam need never have happened.

I believe Dulles later confessed that he thought his delay in sponsoring the Aswan Dam was the greatest mistake of his career as a statesman. I shall always wonder whether I could have convinced him, had he been willing to see me, of the folly of his neglect of Egypt. Surely an alliance with that country could have been won at comparatively little cost. Naturally I feel that my advice might have avoided the loss of countless lives, and enormous treasure. Perhaps more detrimental to our friendships in Europe and the Middle East were our actions when Nasser canceled the lease of the Suez Canal before its expiration date, and we felt impelled to force a settlement of the resulting war.

My service to our government in its foreign relations has sometimes been less formal. As a trustee of the Committee for Economic Development in Washington I aided in the preparation of several position papers. Two had a rather important impact on government policy. The first of these related to economic cooperation with Latin America and had a strong influence on the Kennedy proposal of an Alliance for Progress. The second pertained to the effect on United States trade of the European Common Market as we analyzed it when first proposed by the Treaty of Rome. I acted as chairman of the two sub-committees that produced these papers.

Another unofficial service was my acceptance of the unpaid presidency of Gibraltar Steamship Co., which leased from the U.S. Navy a broadcasting radio station on Swan Island, from which programs were transmitted to Cuba. These were mostly prepared for us by Cuban refugees in the hope of subverting the Castro régime. President Kennedy ordered us to stop these programs after his settlement with Khrushchev at the time of the Cuban missile crisis.

I have also served as chairman of a citizens committee advisory to the Army Corps of Engineers in connection with the Charles River watershed. We were successful in getting a new dam built to control the water level in the basin where floods threatened to cause huge losses to M.I.T., Harvard, and Boston University. Our efforts stimulated great progress in overcoming pollution in the river. The natural areas plan we suggested for protecting the upper parts of the watershed is a prototype much admired in other parts of the country.

Taking the oath of office as Truman's Director of International Security Affairs in the Korean War.

Presiding at a meeting of Truman's International Security Affairs Committee, an interdepartmental group to allocate military and economic aid to our allies during the Korean War. Left to right: Frank Southard, Jr. (Treasury), Maj. Gen. J. H. Burns (Defense), T. D. Cabot (State), Najeeb Halaby (Marshall Plan), Lincoln Gordon (White House).

October 17, 1951

Dear Tom:

Your decision to leave the post with us which you have
filled so ably during the past year, leaves me with a feeling of deep personal as well as official regret.

I appreciate the spirit of public service which prompted
you to undertake, despite the sacrifice it meant to you, the
assignment as Director of International Security Affairs.
Under your pioneering direction the several programs of
United States aid have been coordinated into an effective
unit of our Government's foreign policy, designed to achieve
maximum security for the free world. Your unselfish effort
toward this end has been a valuable contribution to our
progress and a firm foundation upon which Averell Harriman
can build.

My best wishes go with you as you return to private
life.

Sincerely yours,

Dean Acheson

Mr. Thomas D. Cabot, Director,
International Security Affairs,
Department of State.

Americans en route to economic conference of NATO industrialists at Bonn in 1958. Left to right: Milton Lightner, Ward Keener, Charles Percy, David Rockefeller, T. D. Cabot, William Butler, Langbourne Williams, Arthur Houghton, William Burden, and Leo Welch.

With Virginia at a Millwood Hunt Club meet.

Riding with friends in Vermont, 1933.

CHAPTER IX

◦∞◦

The Canoe

HAVING been taught frugality, my siblings and I saved
pennies. We loved boats and had learned to paddle at camps
in Maine and Nova Scotia. Together we bought a canoe. This
we kept at the Cambridge Boat Club on the Charles. At high tide,
in those days before the dam closed the mouth of the river, we
could canoe over the salt marshes which now support many of
the finest buildings of Harvard and M.I.T. We used to explore
all of the lower reaches of the Charles, and once made a tour around
Boston paddling up river to Dedham and through Mother's Brook
to the Neponset, returning to Cambridge via Boston Harbor.
This trip lasted three days, and we came home by streetcar each
night.

In 1910, while I was convalescing from an appendix operation,
my father, who was never a canoeist, took me for a paddle on
the Charles. It was a warm March day with snow still on the banks.
He paddled up river to the old bridge between the abatoir and
the arsenal while I sat among some cushions. In negotiating his
way through the bridge's wooden piles, he managed to upset the
canoe. I ran all the way home after swimming ashore in the icy
water. The conversation was a bit icy, too, when Father returned
from the boathouse and was confronted by Mother.

When a little older, I sometimes shipped my canoe by train
to West Townsend and canoed the Squannacook to West Groton.
There was a bit of rapid water in this river, and I occasionally
got dunked, for I had not yet learned how to handle rapids.

In 1922, Ned Billings, who had canoed with Maine guides as a boy, suggested that he and I try to canoe the rapids of the Quaboag River. We had seen these rapids from the train windows as we returned from New York business trips. It was a dare and I accepted it. At his recommendation, I got some setting poles and rented three canoes and paddles from a Riverside boathouse.

We enlisted our friends Alec Bright, Buck Dumaine, Winsor Gale, and Jim White in the enterprise and agreed to a weekend in early March for the trip. It was customary in those days to work Saturday mornings but in the afternoon we took a train from Riverside with our canoes in the baggage car and arrived at West Brookfield where we started down river in the fading light. One canoe was upset that evening in an easy rapid, but when we got to the inn at Warren we felt confident we could paddle all the way to Hartford next day. The optimism was unwarranted, for within half a mile of leaving Warren next morning, all six of us had overturned in the icy rapids. By the time we got to Palmer, one of the canoes had been broken completely in half and abandoned, and the other two canoes were too badly damaged to be returned. I ended up owning and repairing the two broken ones.

We had at that time an old Chevrolet touring car as the family automobile. Parenthetically, it is interesting to note that it cost me $360 when new. I built a rack over its windshield to support the two canoes. For the next two springs, my wife and I wore out the repaired canoes (and a good many of our friends as well) as we learned how to use a setting pole and keep upright in white water. By then we needed a new canoe and bought a nineteen-foot guide's model made of canvas and white cedar in Skowhegan, Maine. For thirteen years we used that canoe and were never overturned or swamped.

An article I wrote for *Appalachia* in 1928 on canoeing in rapids attracted the attention of the great naturalist, Doctor John Phillips. He got in touch with me with the suggestion that we write a guidebook to all the New England rivers. We did eventually, but it took a lot of exploring. For five years we covered all of the rivers except those in northern Maine that were the preserve of professional guides. The guidebook was published in 1934 and soon sold out. Fortunately the Appalachian Mountain Club now keeps a similar guidebook up to date with occasional new editions. But our publication was the first to popularize canoeing on rapid rivers.

After the war, the Grumman Company asked me to design an ideal canoe to be built of aluminum using the techniques for molding airplane wings that they had developed. Even before the war, I had built a clumsy aluminum canoe of flat sheets, but had to use welded seams to get anything approaching proper curvature. With this new freedom to mold, I came up with a design that has stood the test of time and is closely followed in more than half of the canoes sold today. It has proved easy to handle in quick water and smooth. The ends are fuller and lower to give more buoyancy and less wind resistance than the earlier Indian models. The graceful sheer, modest dead rise, and minimum tumble home combine to provide easy paddling and maneuvering with good stability. Sentimentalists may prefer canoes of more primitive design and less tinny sound when struck, but bark, wood, and canvas lose strength and gain weight with the years and the newer plastics have not found a more popular acceptance.

It is satisfying to note the tremendous increase in interest there has been in white and flat water sports. Today on a good weekend there are scores of canoes and kayaks on every suitable river, but in the early days we saw no one. We did discover, after a couple of years of white water experience, that there was another group of older friends who annually made a trip down the Westfield River and sometimes a trip on the Souhegan. They had been doing this for years before we started, and we made a few trips with them before they quit. This was all before automobiles were used to carry canoes. To run the Westfield, they would ship their canoes by train to Williamsburg in the baggage car and take a Friday evening train to that station, spending the night at an inn. The next morning, a farmer would take the canoes and canoeists in a wagon to Cummington, and they would run the river to a camping spot about a mile below the gorge at West Chesterfield. On Sunday, they would continue to Huntington and ship the canoes back home by train. Similarly, they ran the Souhegan by shipping canoes to Greenville and canoeing to the railroad at Milford. Later when automobiles were the common carriers, it always required a good deal of organizing to get the automobiles from the start at the head to the finish downstream.

With us, canoeing was never a competitive sport, and except in European rivers I have rarely used a kayak. Watching kayak competition today, I am amazed at the skill shown in maneuvering through gates in white water more turbulent than any we coped with even when using a setting pole.

My wife and I did acquire a type of skill which is rarely seen today. This was the technique used by most professional guides in the north woods. For most rapids, she would kneel in the bow of the canoe using a paddle, and I would stand further back with a setting pole. This system does have some advantage over the paddle techniques used today. With the pole one can handle heavier loads and one is better able to find a course through shallow rapids. Also, it is only with a pole that one can go upstream. Today, some of the steep pitches which we portaged or lined down are regularly run in decked canoes or kayaks. This must be exciting. But in our day, when we carried all our camping equipment (and duffel bags were rarely waterproof) a swamped canoe was a much more serious matter than today, for now the occupants wear wetsuits, life jackets, and helmets and have ready transportation by heated automobile if their kit gets wet.

In recent years we have decided that running rapids is a sport for the young, so we rarely canoe. However, when I was nearly eighty, I was invited to canoe for a week on the Upper St. John

River in Northern Maine with a group of young men. They had the canoes flown in by floatplane to the start of our trip. The rapids were not very severe, and I enjoyed the trip immensely, despite being the oldest member of the party by a margin of nearly forty years. The trip was organized by Dickie Saltonstall, an author and ardent conservationist, and included the authors John McPhee and John Kauffman who also write about preserving our heritage of unspoiled land. A delightful account of our tour of that primeval valley, by John McPhee, was in *The New Yorker*. I suspect that I was included in the party because they hoped to persuade Senator Muskie and several Congressmen to come along, and thought the plea that old age would not permit them to face such rigors might be blunted by an octogenarian presence on the trip. A trip down the unspoiled wilderness of the St. John watershed might have persuaded them to oppose the Dickey-Lincoln Project dam that will, if built, flood the valley.

The camping equipment we used was only a fraction of the weight that we carried fifty years ago, and it was far more practical and comfortable. In fact, we were so comfortable on this trip that I am tempted to try one of the guided tours on the famous rivers out West. Perhaps I can still find a chance to try one of the tributaries of the Columbia, the Colorado, or the Rio Grande.

CHAPTER X

꙳

Sailing under the Jolly Roger

SINCE I was a small boy, I have had a strong affinity for salt water. In those days, we spent most of each summer at Beverly Farms. There, at the age of nine I built my first boat from two wooden soap boxes, and in the same year started sailing in a dory owned by older brother Jim.

As I have said, my wife's family had summered on a farm and she was brought up with horses, not boats. In our early married years there was no time for sailing, and it wasn't until our children took to sail that we began to cruise as a family. At Cohasset, when the three older boys were nine, eight and seven, we bought each of them an eight-foot sailing skiff, which were named *Og*, *Gog*, and *Magog* and were raced in the harbor. During the Depression, these inexpensive skiffs were very popular in Cohasset, and each of the boys won a "world championship." In the four summers, 1932 to 1935, we chartered a cruising boat and made voyages to Nantucket, and then to Maine, and to the St. John River in New Brunswick. Each of these chartered vessels had good features and bad. Naturally, this led to our dreaming about building an ideal vessel to own.

In 1936, after a summer abroad, we decided to have John Alden design a yacht to incorporate our ideas, and the keel was laid in December at the Harvey Gamage Yard at South Bristol, Maine. The vessel was a forty-nine-foot auxiliary yawl named *Avelinda*, with a heavy white oak frame, mahogany planking, teak deck, and a seventy-one-foot hollow, wooden mainmast. She had two double state rooms aft and would sleep ten in berths; furthermore, ten could sit at the table in the main cabin. The vessel was a great success and served us well for thirty-eight years until rot made us replace her with a new ketch bearing the same name. We really loved the old yawl. She would no doubt still be serving us, but for the damage done to her in the war when she was used as an icebreaker. Prior to the war, we won a number of ocean races with her; the most notable victory was in the Lambert Cup Race from New London to Marblehead in 1938. After the race, my crew gave me a dinner, and Winsor Gale wrote a ballad, which he read to us. It is in the first person, as if I had written it, but I didn't. He felt the newspaper summary was inadequate. After the dinner, I did write some introductory verses to add to his ballad. (See Appendix.)

We still treasure the silverware we won in that race and several others before the war, but after the war the added weight of duplicate ribs and other repairs made racing the *Avelinda* impractical. So, we added equipment to make cruising more luxurious, such as propane gas for cooking, electric refrigeration, and other modern conveniences. For years we used the vessel for long cruises and a summer home. While our older children were growing up, we had moved each summer to a house in Cohasset given us by uncles, and later to a rented house in Maine. After the war, when our youngest was old enough to join us cruising, we decided to avoid the nuisance of moving our *lares* and *penates*, and lived during the summer months aboard *Avelinda*, when not in Colorado or traveling.

As a boy, my favorite book was Stevenson's *Treasure Island*. I loved to daydream of treasure troves and sailing the Spanish Main. But as a businessman, I had to deal with facts, not fantasy. A businessman can't afford to be gullible. Thus, I tended to think it a myth when first I happened upon a secret of buried gold. It was hardly an "Old Wives' Tale," for it concerned gold buried within my lifetime, and much of the story could be easily verified. Luckily, I didn't altogether dismiss the story, and my appetite was whetted as additional supporting evidence came to my attention. In November of 1951, when I left the State Department, I decided that before returning to business I would take the time to "rescue" this fifty tons of gold buried in earthen pots on a remote island of the Caribbean.

The secret first came to my attention during my presidency of Harvard Travellers Club. It was my duty to find suitable speakers for our monthly dinners, and I heard from a friend that Ed Beckwith, an electrical engineer who had graduated from Harvard ahead of me, had some good color slides of a yachting trip to the Windward and Leeward Islands. I invited him on from New York to speak and to spend the night with us in Weston. His pictures were superb. He had been the navigator on an eighty-foot schooner, skippered by John Archbold, with an amateur crew of twelve. In the course of his account, he mentioned that the real purpose of the trip was to dig for gold on a remote, uninhabited island far from any other land. Naturally, in the question period after his talk he was asked about the location of the gold, but he said this was a secret and refused to say anything more about it. On the way home, I tried again, but learned no more. However, Virginia did a little better. He revealed to her that they left after three days of digging because the island was only eighteen feet high, and they feared they might be washed off of it should a storm come up. From this, it didn't take me very long to identify the island from descriptions in the *Admiralty Sailing Manual*. I guessed it was Aves in the Eastern Caribbean.

Beckwith, a bachelor, usually breakfasted at the Harvard Club, as did I on my frequent trips to New York. I casually asked him about Aves and taken by surprise it was easy to see I had guessed right. Gradually, I learned more, and with bits and pieces from other members of the expedition, I thought I had most of the story of how they happened to make the trip. Also, relevant in-

A steep pitch on the Quabaug River below West Warren. Virginia and I take on a bit of white water.

Using setting pole and paddle on the Contoocook River in a Grumman canoe which I designed.

Rob cooking supper for us on a 1930 canoe trip in Vermont.

Helping a friend to save his canoe on the Westfield River.

Avelinda in the Thames River of New London for the Harvard–Yale crew races in June 1938. See Appendix.

Son Rob sailing his "rooky" *Magog* in 1931.

Avelinda racing New London to Marblehead for the Lambert Cup in June 1938. See Appendix.

When and If in St. Lucia.

Rara Aves in Gozo.

Three Cabot "rookies" compete in a Saturday race at Cohasset, 1933.

The winning team of Cohasset Yacht Club for the "National Rooky Championship" includes three Cabot sons.

Avelinda sailing among the fishing boats of Carver's Harbor, Maine.

formation came from history books, from the archives of the State Department, and from Latin American friends.

Today, Aves Island has shrunk to a sand bar resting on a coral reef and has only a bit of beach grass as vegetation, but in the seventeenth century it was a wooded island several miles in circumference. It has been sinking at a rate estimated by Guillermo Zuloaga as two-tenths of an inch per year, and is now only a narrow crescent about 400 yards long, the nesting place of hundreds of sea tortoises and of thousands of sea birds. Today, it is clearly Venezuelan territory, but until the 1870's its sovereignty was in doubt. The United States has been much criticized in Latin America for the threats it used in forcing a settlement of its claims.

Early in 1854, a brig out of Boston owned by the firm of Sampson and Tappan passing to leeward of this dot on the chart 200 miles from other islands, smelled guano, and putting a boat ashore took samples, which assayed very rich in nitrogen. During the summer, this firm sent several vessels to the island to load guano and took off 7,200 tons. Lang and Delano, also of Boston, sent their vessels and took off 2,000 tons. Then, on October 19 of that year, a Venezuelan gunboat appeared in the roadstead and ordered the Americans to leave. This led to the passage in 1856 of the Guano Act which directs the Secretary of the Navy to take such action as may be necessary to protect the person and operations of any citizen of the United States who lands to collect guano on an uninhabited island more than three miles from other land. The Latins consider this tantamount to armed robbery. Negotiations with respect to Aves Island were delayed by the Civil War and by arbitration between other claimants, but in 1870, after Venezuela had established its claim against England, Holland, Spain, and France, a settlement was negotiated by the United States minister in Caracas which resulted in Venezuela paying the United States $130,000 in full settlement of the latter's claims. This was used to indemnify Samson and Tappan by a payment of $105,000 and Lang and Delano by a payment of $25,000.

That Aves had then become Venezuelan was well known among Latin Americans and must have been known to Jose Ignacio Andrade, President of Venezuela, when he lost a revolution to Cypriano Castro in 1899. Dispatches in the newspapers of the time describe how Andrade, as his defeat became imminent, collected all the private and church gold he could find and, with the gold remaining in the national treasury, loaded it on mules and took it from Caracas to the seaport of LaGuaira, fleeing from there into exile on a small schooner.

It was easy for one to verify that he had fled into exile and that many heavy earthen pots had accompanied him, but I was left with a good deal of doubt that there really was any fifty tons of gold or that it had actually been buried. Revolutions are not apt to be lost while there is gold with which to hire mercenaries, and it is tempting for a dictator and his retinue to use for their living expenses in exile all they have been able to save.

The story as told me by Beckwith and others is that a banker named Fairchild was visited in New York by a Latin named Perez who identified himself as the son-in-law of Andrade and offered to reveal the location of this horde of gold if Fairchild would organize a party to recover it. The expedition was to be composed entirely of reliable amateur gentlemen who would give him (Perez) a promise of sixty percent on delivery of the gold in New York. Fairchild, after some investigation, decided he couldn't take time off himself but interested John Archbold, a Standard Oil heir, in the project. With shovels, picks, and dynamite, they sailed from Essex, Connecticut, in an eighty-foot auxiliary schooner in mid-winter of 1932. It was a stormy passage and on the way to the tropics they met a series of storms, finally losing their rudder and having to be towed into San Juan for repairs. They had expected Perez to join them in Charlotte Amalie, but, arriving late, they found him unwilling to accompany the party to Aves Island, perhaps for fear that Venezuelan officials might arrest him if he were discovered in Venezuelan waters. However, he did produce a map of the island which located the treasure relative to the point where a coral reef disappeared below a sand beach. There they dug without success, possibly because the subsidence of the island in the thirty-five intervening years had substantially changed this point of departure.

For years the party considered returning to Aves. Presumably Perez was dead. But they needed a device to locate the gold. Beckwith, in collaboration with Doctor Fisher, devised an electronic doodlebug that depended on dielectric anomalies and was the prototype of the modern mine detector. They never got around to a return to Aves, but Beckwith did spend several vacations testing his device where there were other rumors of treasure and the resulting adventures would fill a book. I recall only two. Early in the use of his doodlebug he was arrested as a spy using an electronic device to communicate with counter-revolutionaries from the Isle of Pines. He got off by appealing to the greed of the police who led him to a site which triggered his device. After a night of digging, the metal proved to be a large brass cannon. This experience taught him to seek permission from the local and national governments as well as from the landowner. Later, in the town of Trinidad on the south coast of Cuba, he thought his permits in order and was seeking a cache of gold in an area which had been dug over by earlier seekers when his device gave signals on both sides of a big tree. He decided the gold must have been buried when the tree was a sapling. He dug all day, but it was such hard work he decided to employ help. This, of course, spread the news and a crowd collected. Deep under the huge roots of the tree they came upon a stout oaken keg. Before he was able to extract it from the embrace of the roots, a sheriff appeared and charged him with trespassing. His permit, it seems, was signed not by the true owner of the property but only by a tenant. Poor Beckwith had to stand by and see the keg opened to reveal gold coins worth more then $40,000. He got not a one.

So from time to time I told friends of my hope of finding buried treasure and humored them with discussions of how we might proceed. Obviously we couldn't land a bulldozer. Secrecy seemed important. The claim of the finder of a trove is not good against its burier nor against anyone from whom it may have been stolen, nor against the sovereign government of the territory in which it is found. I practiced with war surplus mine detectors and found that their limit was about six feet for a man-sized chunk of metal. Other devices did little better and were even more difficult to carry. The game became as exciting as the prize. If at first my secret talks were tongue in cheek, as the years passed they became more than half believed. There was no difficulty in finding conspirators who wanted to visit Aves. The *Avelinda* was available. The only problem was to find the time. When I was about to leave the State Department, it seemed that a vacation was in order and I decided it was then or never.

Virginia happened to mention to Bea Patton that I was thinking of taking our *Avelinda* to the Caribbean. Bea, the widow of General George Patton, suggested that I take her schooner, *When and If*, and that she and Virginia join us somewhere in the British West Indies after our treasure hunt was over. She even offered to provision the vessel for a cruise of three months.

When and If was a larger and sturdier vessel than *Avelinda*. Built for George and Bea in 1938 when he was a lieutenant colonel and expecting soon to retire, she could easily carry a concentrated cargo of fifty tons. They intended to take her on a cruise around the world. The war and his glorious campaigns intervened; he was killed in a jeep in Germany soon after the fighting ceased. In the busy thirteen years since she was built, they had no chance to use the schooner except for occasional short, one-day trips. Although thoroughly seaworthy she had not been tested in stormy weather and this led to some discomfort.

So, while I was still in Washington, Bea provisioned the vessel with everything we could conceivably need for comfort, convenience, and enjoyment. This included more than a ton of canned goods and 144 rolls of toilet paper. On the second day of my return from Washington, I came aboard with an all-male crew of friends, and we sailed from Manchester, Massachusetts, into the wintry Atlantic. It took us seven days to reach Bermuda and the weather was stormy most of the way. We soon discovered that the electric wiring had been badly connected, so that even when switched off there were hot wires on both masts which short-circuited to the rigging when wet. This meant that touching any metal above deck gave one a thirty-two-volt shock—not enough to be dangerous—but startling, especially when wet with salt spray. The other discomfort was a bit more serious; the bilge pumps did not reach to the bottom of the bilge and couldn't remove the last barrel of bilgewater. This remainder sloshed back and forth synchronously with the roll of the vessel until, hitting the shelf below the deck, it would spray clear across the cabin into the opposite bunk wetting everything in between. For seven days nothing was dry in the vessel. All of the labels on that ton of canned goods were washed off. Thereafter, when we expected pork and beans, we got lobster newburg or vice versa. Arriving at Bermuda we shoveled out the toilet paper, rewired the lighting circuits, extended the intake hose of the smaller bilge pump and after thirty-six hours in Hamilton, were ready to depart for the Virgin Islands.

It took us less than five days for the nine-hundred-mile run from Bermuda to Charlotte Amalie. We averaged nine knots running before a norther with only a staysail set and every man tethered while on deck. Actually, we never took a heavy sea on board, but neither could we ever sight sun, moon, or star. This made for an exciting landfall. Fortunately, with dead reckoning guiding us, we were able to recognize the hills of St. Thomas through the driving rain. We rounded the island to the shelter of Charlotte Amalie harbor and the welcome of a tropical resort.

Despite the storms and general sogginess there were many pleasant things to remember about this leg of our journey. We had three lawyers in the crew and they came with typewriter, foolscap paper, blue binders, and legal seals for the elaborate articles of agreement we prepared. These we all signed in blood as becomes proper buccaneers. By these articles we pledged to form a Liberian corporation controlled by a charitable foundation. This chartered the vessel and agreed to pay each member of the crew a modest stipend plus one percent of any surplus from the proceeds of our success. A larger sum plus two percent of the surplus would go to Bea Patton. The gold would be taken to a vault we had arranged for in Cuba, because it was illegal to bring gold into the United States, and from there it would be sold in the best market (probably Montevideo) for conversion into U.S. currency. We were all to be trustees of the charitable foundation and meet once a year to decide on the charities to receive the income. We even decided which types of charities would be given preference in early distributions, and toasts were drunk to the best ideas. It was an able crew and a stout vessel and except for the helmsman, we spent most of each watch comfortably in the doghouse where there was always an earnest discussion in progress of how we would spend each pot of gold.

At Charlotte Amalie there were crew changes and signals to be made, then we continued southward with pleasant weather. It took two days to reach the approach to Aves Island. We were now in Venezuelan waters, with little chance that we could claim any legitimacy for our mission, so we hoisted the Jolly Roger to the masthead with a cannon salute acknowledged by squawks from booby birds and gulls. Before dawn of the third day, I was able to get five star altitudes which placed us just five miles to the west of the island.

It was a nerve-wracking approach in the heavy seas of the strong trade winds. From the deck of the vessel one could see ahead only on the crest of each wave and it was hard to distinguish the surf of the low island from other breakers all about us. We dared not come nearer than half a mile of the beach. Where the lead-line showed only two-and-a-half fathoms we anchored. Between us and the island the huge waves coming around each end of the crescent would meet in a pile of water that seemed insurmountable. From high on the mast we studied the situation and decided that an approach toward the northern end of the island would be the safest. We had only one boat, a twelve-foot lapstrake mahogany tender. We decided that three of us would make the first attempt to get ashore, taking with us the water-proofed doodlebug, a pick, and two shovels. The Bemis brothers, Gregg and Alan, were selected for their experience in surf and the skipper for his experience with the doodlebug. Bailey Aldrich, the mate, was to remain aboard in command.

The landing was a near disaster saved only by the skill of Gregg as coxswain. The oarsmen jumped out too soon to hold the tender from receding with the wave it had ridden. They found themselves in water too deep to get a foothold, but the next wave broke further out which saved the boat from broaching. After getting ashore and recovering from the exertion, we switched on the doodlebug, waited for the tubes to warm up, balanced the circuit, and started up the slope of the beach. We hadn't yet gained the first beach grass when the galvanometer needle jumped to the top of the scale. Without further study we shut off the device and set to work with pick and shovels. It was hard digging and within half an hour all three of us had blisters and the hole was scarcely four feet deep. So again we turned on and balanced our device. There was no reaction at the bottom of the hole but nearby was another response which we studied more carefully. It was obviously from a small piece of metal near the surface and we soon found it to be only a shard or splinter from a steel bomb. Within a few minutes we had found a whole collection of shallowly buried shards. Evidently Aves had been used as a target for bombers. These frustrated every attempt to study what might be buried deeper.

In the course of the day, all members of the crew landed on

and was blown onto West Beach. On hearing the news I ran to the beach and felt sure the vessel would be destroyed pounding on the hard sand. It was only when my mother promised she would finance the repairs that my sobs abated.

My second experience with a tornado was at the start of my sophomore year at Harvard. The Billings family invited me to a house party at Vineyard Haven. Learning that Virginia was to be there, I quickly accepted. One day we all planned to take a hired catboat to Menemsha Bight for a picnic. Mrs. Billings and another lady were to come by motor and meet us there. It was hot with little wind and the single-cylinder engine of the catboat became overheated and wouldn't run. In consequence we arrived late at the rendezvous and were not through with our picnic lunch until about 4:30. Black clouds were collecting and it was obvious that we were in for a squall. So all the girls were piled into the Billings touring car while the boys undertook to help the catboat's owner get it back to Vineyard Haven. We were somewhere in Vineyard Sound when the squall struck. Although we had seen it coming and got the sails furled, once it struck, all we could do was crouch behind the gunwales, beg mercy of the wind, and bail for dear life as waves slopped on board. It soon rained so hard that we couldn't see and had no idea where the wind was taking us. For a while we managed to get the engine going and headed into wind and wave. Night fell and the engine failed, overheated despite the pouring rain. We had glimpses of lights but couldn't identify them. Finally, shortly before midnight, we were blown onto an unknown beach. We all got ashore safely and carried the anchor up the beach in the hope of saving the catboat. Drenched, cold, and miserable we huddled together. Presently, someone thought he saw a light up the beach. We walked toward it and came to the summer house of Senator William Butler. We were at Lambert Cove just west of West Chop. The senator greeted us in his dressing-gown, soon had a fire going and hot buttered rum for all of us, and as the storm abated, he sent a servant to the Billings' house with word that we were safe and sound.

I have had only one other close brush with a tornado and that was when rowing with my niece on Lake Cochituate near Weston. We had no trouble getting ashore but were hard put to decide whether to take shelter in the trees and risk being killed by falling limbs or to crouch in the open and risk being blown away. I have seen another tornado with an awesome black funnel when flying over Texas, but it was easy to see how to dodge trouble and stay away from it. We learned next day it had destroyed most of the town of Lefors.

That story of the hot buttered rum reminds me of another time years later when it was I who acted as a Good Samaritan to some cold, wet waifs. Virginia and I were living in a rented house near her sister Linda Perkins in Southwest Harbor, Maine. Virginia was caring for our infant son, Ned, and couldn't be away overnight. The members of the Northeast Harbor Yacht Club were planning their annual cruise and invited *Avelinda* to join. Their plan was to race to Prettymarsh where the younger members who were racing in open knockabouts would camp on the shore, and parents sleep on board the larger yachts. I persuaded Virginia and her sister to adopt a plan that would let us join the cruise, namely that Virginia and I would race our vessel and Linda would motor to Prettymarsh in our car, have supper with us, and spend the night aboard while Virginia drove the car home and returned next morning for the race back; Linda would then return home in the car.

We won the race to Prettymarsh and Linda was there to greet us. After dinner it started to rain. Virginia had left us and Linda and I had retired, when there was a knocking on the topside of the vessel. I went on deck to find a young man and five teenage girls in a dinghy asking for help. They were all sopping wet and blue with cold. Somehow, they had upset the dinghy and been dumped into the icy Maine water with all their food, blankets, and spare clothing. We got them aboard, found them such dry clothing as there was on *Avelinda*, rolled them into dry blankets, and put them in bunks with mugs of hot buttered rum. We gave them breakfast in the morning. After they had said good-bye, it occurred to me that we hadn't explained that Linda was my sister-in-law and they probably thought "Mrs. Perkins" and I were "living in sin."

Alcohol is good for a chill only if one has come in from the cold. It opens the capillary blood vessels and warms the skin but this dissipates the body warmth faster and can be disastrous if the exposure to cold continues. Under the conditions cited above, hot buttered rum was ideal.

Hurricanes cover a wider area and are harder to avoid. Undoubtedly the most costly storm ever to hit New England was the hurricane of 1938. I missed it by being in New York but had some of the worry and lots of the grief. Our daughter Linda, age nine, was riding her pony in Weston and took refuge in a neighbor's house. I flew home and arrived before we had any word that she was safe. Our place was a shambles and my wife in tears. It was a full day before Linda reached us. We had no electricity or telephone for three weeks and lost 165 shade trees of ten inches minimum diameter on our thirteen acres. It took months to clear up the mess. I used some of *Avelinda*'s cordage, blocks, and other tackle which were invaluable in the immense job of restoring almost unaided some order to our home acres in Weston.

Over the years we have seen some mighty big storms at sea, several of which could be called hurricanes. Even in large vessels storms are dangerous. On our trip to Santo Domingo by steamer in 1930 we ran into a major storm which broke much of the furniture. The piano, which was lashed to a stanchion, got loose and broke itself and everything else in the saloon. Our trunk got loose in the state room and would have destroyed itself and us had I not got it fast with the use of belts, neckties, stockings, and everything else I could find. A few years later while returning from Europe on a large liner, a rogue wave crashed on the forecastle killing four seamen.

But the highest winds I have ever encountered were on the old *Avelinda*. She rode out the famous hurricane of 1938 at her mooring in Cohasset Harbor without any damage. No one was on board. In Hurricane Carol in 1954, I was not so lucky. My family were all away, wife and youngest son in Germany, and I had invited a young friend, his wife and two small sons to cruise with me. They were all from the Middle West. I became aware that they were rank novices when they arrived at the dock with a steamer trunk. We struggled to get it into the dinghy and then I asked my friend to get in so that he could help me load it onto the moored vessel. He stepped onto the dinghy's gunwale and "did the splits" falling between dinghy and float. This half filled the dinghy and soaked the contents of the trunk.

After finally getting the party and its kit aboard and partially dried, we sailed to a secluded cove. The next morning it was raining and the two small boys were complaining that there was nothing to do. The tide was low, so I suggested we go clamming. We got a nice bucket of clams, but they wanted a chowder rather than steamed clams. I had no salt pork or onion, and the lady needed some other supplies for her recipe so we headed out across Penobscot Bay to get them. I had been so busy as skipper, host, and steward that I hadn't turned on the radio. There was little wind or sea and only a slight drizzle, so we were carrying full sail. After a while, there were some unheralded puffs which began to prove worrisome to the passengers, and I lowered the main. With shortened sail the vessel began to roll and the passengers all felt seasick. They retired below leaving me alone on deck, but this didn't seem troublesome as I was used to solo sailing. We were making slow progress under shortened sail so I started the engine. Soon the puffs became much harder and the wind veered to dead ahead. Fearing the fury of the gale would shred the remaining sails, I lowered jib and mizzen. Even with my large propeller and using full power the rapid increase in the wind and rising seas soon made the vessel somewhat unmanageable. The spindrift cut my face so that I had to keep my head below the coaming of the cockpit. By lashing the helm with about fifteen degrees of starboard rudder, I found that I could hold the vessel at about fifty degrees from the eye of the wind to starboard. With the centerboard down she seemed to be drifting approximately at right angles to the wind and parallel to the leeward shore which was only a mile away. Only occasionally could I get glimpses of this shore through the spume. Even under bare poles, the vessel was heeling with the lee rail under water most of the time. There was little I could do except crouch on the floor of the cockpit with my face shielded from the sting of the spindrift, with the wheel lashed and my hand on the engine throttle, adjusting it with each gust in an attempt to keep the vessel from falling off the wind or broaching. I was powerless to tack, fighting to keep off the lee shore, and always cursing my own stupidity in setting out without listening to a weather report, risking so many innocent souls who had had the faith to entrust themselves to my care.

All of the hatches were well secured and there was no means of communicating with the passengers in the cabin. I really couldn't imagine the fears of someone who had never been at sea and had no idea what to expect. After six hours of this worrisome condition I caught a glimpse to leeward of the docks of Searsport and realized we must be in the lee of Sears Island. There seemed to be some abatement in the wind and sea. With my seaman's knife in my teeth I managed to crawl forward and cut away the 125-pound yachtsman-type anchor which I always carried at the cathead, letting the whole of my forty fathoms of half-inch chain run out to the bitter end. The anchor held the vessel until the storm abated.

When I was able to get below, the conditions there were frightful to behold, and my seasick passengers must have had a dreadful time. I turned on the radio and the first words I heard told me that the main antenna tower in Boston had blown down. This was followed by stories of other disasters. The center of the hurricane had evidently passed not far to the west of my position so that I was in the quadrant of maximum winds that reached approximately one hundred miles per hour.

I doubt that my friends ever put to sea again. When we got ashore I tried to make up by offering a walking trip in the woods and hills of eastern Maine, but this was far from adequate compensation for the hardship they had suffered.

The strongest winds and heaviest rains I have ever seen were in Hurricane Edna two weeks later. We had plenty of warning and were securely anchored, but the center of this great cyclonic storm passed directly over us with winds officially recorded at 130 miles per hour. Twelve inches of rain fell, sinking the nearby fishing boats with their open cockpits. Although we were in no mortal danger, the fear that we might drag our anchors onto the shore, as well as the shriek of the wind and the vibrations of the whole ship left us near nervous exhaustion.

In an earlier year, we met a gale of almost hurricane force when caught at sea, having sailed from Massachusetts to the southeast coast of Nova Scotia. Then, too, we had a young, miserably seasick crew closed in below deck. Through a terrible night Bill Binnian and I fought the storm and tried to determine where we were being carried. Finally, in driving rain and southerly squalls we found the Sambro Lightship and came into Halifax Harbor at 2:00 A.M. running at eight knots under bare poles. Even then, and all morning, we couldn't get ashore, for there was too much wind to bring the vessel to a dock or to use our tender.

Years later, in the new *Avelinda*, a forty-two foot Whitby ketch bought in 1975, we were caught at sea by the tail of an unpredicted hurricane on our way from Newfoundland to Nova Scotia. Before wind and wave, we came into the cove of the yacht yard at Baddeck, scaring onlookers. When we rounded up to two heavy anchors with hardly a yard to spare, it is reported that women screamed.

Several times we have hove to for hours while riding heavy storms at sea. In Malibar 13 off Baracoa, Cuba, we once rode out a Force 10 norther for twenty-six hours under trisail with the helm lashed.

Besides our cruises nearer home, we have made seven in the Caribbean, covering pretty thoroughly the Greater and Lesser Antilles. We also have had cruises in the Mediterranean, mostly among the islands of the Aegean and Ionian Seas, and one in the northern European waters. In small yachts and large, we have experienced the strong winds of the mistral, the meltemi, and the khamsin and have enjoyed visits to the isles of Greece and Italy. Europe has much to offer the yachtsman, and we wish we had found the time to explore its waters more thoroughly.

Even after becoming somewhat experienced as a seaman, I have had a number of mishaps due not to storms, but to foolhardiness or negligence. When we first got the original *Avelinda*, I took her into Cobscook Bay on a rising tide and was persuaded by a more experienced friend to take the vessel through the rapids west of Falls Island. He told me to hug the point to port lest I be carried onto the ledge below. Too late I realized that the water was running over a ledge just off the end of the point falling at least six feet into the swirl below. We couldn't possibly have gone to the right around the ledge. With an instant decision I called for full left rudder to hit the vee of water flowing between ledge and point. We slipped through without touching, but the backwave covered our deck and filled the cockpit.

Another time we anchored just at dusk in Moose Snare Cove at dead low tide and let out enough chain, but there being no wind it landed on top of the anchor. After midnight we were awakened with a terrific yank and sound of rushing water. Running on deck we found ourselves in a heavy rapids with trees overhead and soon realized that with the rising tide the anchor had been picked up and had caught in an abandoned mill-race at the head of the cove. We couldn't get the anchor free nor climb the rapids under full power, but with the chain winched up bar-tight we finally yanked free and drifted backwards into the mill pond. Later examination revealed that a loop of chain had fouled around one fluke of the anchor and the other fluke had caught a heavy wooden timber left in the mill-race when the mill was destroyed. The only damage was to the anchor itself. We had pulled it until it bent a full ninety degrees to let go.

Another interruption to a placid night on *Avelinda* occurred when we nearly sank at anchor in a freah water cove of the St. John River. We had backed off of a weed-covered mudbank shortly before anchoring, and this apparently unscrewed the stuffing box of the propeller shaft. We didn't notice it until after midnight when in a restless moment my hand slipped off the bunk into cold water. Fortunately the pumps were still operative. We soon pumped clear and fixed the leak, but had to spend all the next day drying out everything stored below bunk level.

Perhaps the most dramatic incident in the life of the old *Avelinda* was in Haycock Harbor. This is our favorite "gunk-hole" in Maine and is entered by a very narrow passage between needle-sharp rocks to a small basin with hardly room for a yacht to swing. There is a cliff to starboard with high trees above, and it had always been my practice to anchor close to the cliff where the water is deepest. One summer day we entered at noon shortly before high tide and went ashore to play a game of scouting in the woods. In the middle of the game there was a cry as someone noticed the mast was awry. It quickly became apparent that the vessel had swung her stern against the cliff as the tide turned. We found the skeg of her keel had caught in a crack. We couldn't get her free. The tide was falling with some eighteen feet to go. We feared the vessel would fall over and break apart. The afternoon was spent getting her thoroughly fastened against swing-

ing or tipping with the falling tide. The bow was securely anchored and every masthead halyard was tied to limbs high in the
trees above. Soon after dark it began to rain. There was a summer cloudburst and the downpour continued until after midnight.
We hadn't marked the trees to which our halyards were fastened,
and it took us many hours of climbing in the dark in sopping wet
clothes to locate and disengage the fastenings. Fortunately, at
1:00 A.M. the tide was just high enough for us to haul the un-
damaged vessel free from her posture of "tail in the crack" by
kedging with the anchor.

During her hours of peril, life in the vessel was not easy. There
must have been a forward cant of nearly forty-five degrees at low
tide. It seemed that everything movable, including the bilge water,
had slid into the forecastle. It took the rest of the night to clean
up the mess.

In the Caribbean, too, we have had some excitement. Once when
approaching the island of Nevis in a large schooner yacht, there
was a terrific bump. I thought we must have hit a whale, but there
was no evidence of anything near us and we were clearly off sound-
ings. We were completely puzzled as to what had happened until we reached the anchorage and learned that a severe earthquake
had destroyed parts of the town that day.

Some years later when approaching this same island we again
encountered trouble. We had chartered a sixty-foot yawl from
English Harbor at Antigua. It was December and the yawl had
been sailed from England the previous June and was laid-up at
the dock ever since. The boatswain and steward who came with
the vessel were supposed to be experienced so we assumed, in-
correctly, that they had sailed her before and that she was well
found and ready for sea. We had a fair wind to Nevis and as we approached the island after dark we saw that the lighthouse on the
south coast was not being used. But this presented no problem
as we could see the headland by starlight. We sailed around the
island until we were opposite the lights of Charlestown on the

lee side. Then, with headsails furled, we luffed toward shore. I had called for a lead line to be ready, but they couldn't find it. We drifted, with sails flapping, waiting for a jury line to be improvised. This took some time. After deciding we were close enough I gave orders to let go the anchor. The chain just started to run before it immediately stopped. It had jammed on the gypsyhead with the 200-pound anchor just below the surface of the water. The only other anchor we had was stowed below decks under some other gear. The crew went below to disentangle it. The drifting vessel now grounded gently on sand. I started the diesel engine and pushed the clutch handle to reverse. It had no effect. I opened the throttle and the vessel surged forward putting her hard aground. I stopped the engine to have a look and found that the clutch had rusted so badly that it had frozen in the ahead position. I disconnected the controls from the clutch, put it into reverse and pressed the starter. There was a flash and a smell of burning rubber. The starter relay had frozen in a short circuit position. Now with batteries dead, we had no lights except a small electric torch. The second anchor was finally unraveled and brought on deck. We lowered it into the tender and rowed seaward with the spare rode attached. We dropped it in deep water and two of us tried to pull it home while waiting for the tackle to be rigged to give us the power we hoped would pull us off. With two of us pulling and without any tackle the rode parted. The Manila hemp was completely rotted. Now we had no anchor, no power, and no way to get free.

There were shouts from the shore and small boats began appearing in the darkness. Dozens of natives swarmed aboard, shouting in an indistinguishable Papaimento dialect. We couldn't communicate over the hubbub, nor distinguish one from another in the darkness. We didn't know if they had come to help us or pick us clean. A slight surge came around the island from the windward side and pushed us shoreward. After some minutes, a launch appeared. Its skipper seemed as confused as we by the shouting.

Somehow, a big Manila line from the launch was brought aboard and made fast to our after bits to pull us seaward. In its mad rushes, the launch was like a huge fish fighting to be free, but the yanking was to no avail. With a final jerk the big rope parted.

The rescue launch anchored and its captain came aboard to discuss our predicament. His name was Price. He spoke quietly and with intelligence and said that he had been sent to aid us by the Crown representative. There was no tide at Nevis to help us and the surge was obviously pushing us ever deeper onto the sand. I went ashore with Price to look for the only other boat that was supposed to be on the island, a privately-owned ferry that was larger and more powerful than his launch. Meanwhile, Saturday after-midnight parties were in full swing. We stopped before a dark cottage and a prognathous black giant answered our knock. He was Captain Wells of the ferry boat.

I had been thinking of heavy salvage claims, and I regret to say that I mistook Captain Wells' reticence for cupidity. My inquiries as to possible charges were only met with a toothy grin and something to the effect that he would try to help but didn't know what we needed.

It took some time to assemble a crew and get his ferry under weigh. We took aboard a huge wire cable carried by a dozen men and made it fast to the yawl, but Captain Wells had no more success than Captain Price, for the yawl had evidently inched shoreward during the delay. At 3:00 A.M., we called off further attempts until daylight. We spent the rest of the night recovering our lost anchor astern and rigging a tackle to hoist the heavy bower anchor and free the chain on the gypsyhead. Now with two anchors placed astern and new ropes leading to the sheet winches, we could keep the vessel from moving further shoreward. At dawn, we decided that only by careening to tip the keel could we free the vessel from the sand. And so, with a heavy line to the masthead, the big ferry boat pulled down the mast and raised the keel so that the stern anchors could pull the hull into deeper water. It took the rest of the day to repair a broken spreader aloft, recharge the batteries, rebuild the starter relay, and fix a jury rig to control the clutch.

In the evening I went ashore with a heavy heart to pay my bills. Dozens of the natives had spent their Sunday helping us. How could I tell in the dim light which was which of the dark faces or to whom I was indebted. I sought the help of the Crown representative. My faith in humanity was soon restored. These poor people had really learned the Golden Rule. Everywhere I was met with apologies for the mishap and refusal to take payment. In the end I settled the bill by giving the island a clock with chimes to help get the children to school on time.

CHAPTER XII

Skiing

ALTHOUGH my sailing career started at an early age, my skiing career started even earlier. On Christmas day in 1902 I was given my first pair of skis. They were made of pine with leather toestraps. I used these for sliding in the suburban yards of Cambridge and Belmont. In 1907 I got ash skis with proper bindings and started skiing in earnest. This came about because my father was persuaded to buy two tickets to a charity exhibition of ski jumping at the Twin Elm Spring Farm in Lexington. I went with a friend, Delano Potter, by streetcar. We carried our toestrap skis with us. As we stood against the rope barrier at the foot of the hill munching our lunches, one of the Norwegian jumpers stopped to speak to me. I couldn't understand his broken English, but I gathered he was being critical of my skis. He wrote with a pencil stub on my lunch bag the word *"Huitfeld."* The next day, when my uncle Frank Moors came to lunch, I told him of the incident, handing him the word torn from my lunch bag. A few weeks later there arrived from New York a fine new pair of imported skis with steel and leather bindings similar to the ones used by professionals. Not long after this John Martin and Alec Bright also acquired some proper equipment and soon we were all learning to make crude Telemark and Christiania turns. I kept these skis until after our marriage when I sought better skiing. It was then that we joined the Laurentian Lodge Club at Shawbridge, Quebec, where we skied with Canadians, and enjoyed both downhill and cross-country skiing with the best early 1920's equipment available.

Skiing

In 1924 I was one of a group from the Appalachian Mountain Club who were to improve the footpath over the Wapack Range so that it could be used as a ski trail. After Christmas I led a party of the Harvard Mountaineering Club on a two-day, cross-country ski trip over the trail from Russell Station to Ashburnham. As we descended the summit of Barrett Mountain, Bob Balch, then a Harvard freshman, fell on the sharp stub of a shrub and received what appeared to be a minor puncture wound. He fainted from trauma and we had the difficult job of carrying him through two miles of woods in deep powder snow to the Wilder Farm in East Rindge. The local doctor found no cause for the trauma and prescribed rest. Fortunately the elderly Mrs. Wilder had been trained as a nurse in her girlhood. After the doctor left she said she thought the situation was getting serious and called the Balch family in Boston. The young man's uncle, Franklin Balch, was a famous surgeon. He rushed to Rindge in his Pierce Arrow to bring the boy to the Massachusetts General Hospital where they found a punctured colon that would have been fatal but for emergency surgery.

Later that year I led another group of Harvard skiers to Pinkham Notch and we nearly lost another young Harvard man who got separated from the party in a dense cloud on the ice-covered summit of Mount Washington. I shudder to think how close we came to a catastrophe for which I would have been blamed. We found him almost frozen after a search that endangered all of us, and we got him into the Camden Hut on the summit and revived him by the heat of a stove. After a few hours rest he was able to get down the mountain with some help from the group.

I have recorded how we skied in the Alps in the summer of 1926. While there we saw skis with steel edges and cable bindings and I soon acquired a new pair. The following spring I was one of a group from the Appalachian Mountain Club to spend a week at Chimney Pond on the slopes of Mount Katahdin in Maine, and made the first ski ascent of that mountain. Two years later, in 1929, Fritz Steuri came from Grindlewald and showed us how far behind Europe we really were in our skiing skills. In that year we introduced our three sons to the sport.

A mechanical ski lift was built at the Laurentian Lodge Club in 1930. I think it was the first in America. Alec Bright and I were there at the start of operation. It was a primitive rope tow and didn't make a profit until moved to Woodstock, Vermont. The following year we opened the Taft Trail on Cannon Mountain which the Duke von Leuchtenberg had built with funds collected by Kate Peckett. The ski school at Sugar Hill was then in full swing with Sig Buchmayer, Harold Paumgarten, and Sepp Lanz as teachers.

Then in the winter of 1933, Virginia and I made the first of many trips to Europe for skiing. We visited the more famous Alpine resorts spending about a week each at St. Anton, St. Mortiz, Davos, and Murren. Our techniques improved immeasurably from contact with the better Alpine skiers. Also, in the early 1930's we were invited by George Cranmer on behalf of the state of Colorado to visit West Portal, now Winter Park, to report on the potential of the Berthoud Pass area for a ski resort. We recommended it highly. In 1936, Cranmer asked us to visit Aspen. After four days of climbing and sliding on narrow wood roads we reported unfavorably—an error our friends who ski with us nowadays on the superb runs carved from these woods don't let us forget.

After Christmas in 1936 we were at the opening of the new ski resort at Sun Valley. Getting to Sun Valley was an amusing experience. I was in Texas on business and had made arrangements for my wife to come directly to Idaho from Boston by train, promising to meet her somewhere en route. My railroad friends predicted no problem in getting from the Texas Panhandle to a junction in Wyoming, where I could meet her train. After my arrival in Texas I was told that if I wanted to make the connection I would have to spend a day in Denver unless I wanted to

tions at that time seemed especially hazardous, for there was considerable wind slab over several feet of unconsolidated powder snow. I felt the guide unduly reckless and had several arguments with him about the dangerous conditions. On our fifth day at the lodge, we climbed Mount Richardson on skis, planning a descent by the snowfilled, north-facing cirque. When we were on top, I spoke again of the avalanche danger and suggested to the guide that we stick to the ridge, but he scoffed telling us that he would lead and his clients were to follow and that I should go last. It was not very steep, but two of the novice skiers were afraid to make downhill turns and started to descend by short traverses and kick-turns. As it was getting late, the guide shouted for them to hurry. He then shouted for me to ski on down past them, which I did. I stopped on the ridge near those who had come down ahead of me and somewhat above the guide who was on the slope waving his poles and shouting encouragement to the two novices. I had just told Virginia to come higher onto the ridge when the whole face of the cirque broke and slid down into the trees below with a force that uprooted trees. My eyes were on my wife lest she be buried, but she was carried only a few yards and able to dig herself out. One novice, who had started the slide by making a kick-turn, was able to free himself. But still missing were the guide and the other novice. We immediately sent Virginia, who was the best woman skier, down to the lodge for help, including shovels and blankets. The rest of the party started probing with ski poles. Presently, the ringed end of a pole was seen on the slope above us. It didn't release when pulled, and we dug to find it fastened to the wrist of the buried novice. We dug her out unconscious and revived her with mouth-to-mouth resuscitation. We continued to probe feverishly, searching for the guide. After another hour, when it was getting dark, we thought our probing had found something at a depth of about six feet. Digging with hands and ski tips, we came to a man's head, and Roy Little, who deserves enormous praise for his heroism, dove into the hole to blow air into the victim's lungs. It took us one more hour to get the guide's body disengaged from his skis, which were buried twelve feet below the surface of the snow. The temperature was below zero by this time, and if there was any life left in the body, we had no way to revive it, for the first helper to arrive brought no blanket, and by the time a toboggan reached us the corpse was frozen.

I have seen many other avalanches which were not fatal, and will speak of one which gave us quite a scare. In motoring over Loveland Pass west of Denver, before the tunnel was built, we were going along at about forty miles an hour when suddenly an avalanche hit us from above. It pushed our car across the road but luckily not over the edge. We were completely buried, all but for the top of one downhill window. We were able to open it and crawled through this narrow gap. Fortunately, our forward motion had brought us close to the side of the avalanche. We dug the car out using skis for shovels and continued our drive to Aspen. It was not until the next day that the road was cleared for traffic so that others could follow us.

Avalanches are a serious hazard to skiers when away from the frequented slopes, just as thin ice is dangerous to lone skaters. Before skiing became popular my mother's brothers used to take us youngsters on river skating expeditions. We always carried a rope and several times I've been pulled out of holes in the ice. On our best trip, we took the train to North Billerica and skated up the Concord and Sudbury Rivers to the Cochituate reservoirs, crossing these to the trolley car which took us to South Natick. From there we skated down the Charles River to the railroad station in West Roxbury. I still have tender toes from the frostbite I got on one of these trips and they sometimes trouble me when skiing.

Weekend ski trips with our children were frequent in the winters prior to their service in World War II and skiing has continued to be a favorite sport since the war for all the family. It has contributed to the togetherness of our children and grandchildren. Nowadays we often have some of them with us on our skiing trips. We have spent the Christmas–New Year holidays in Aspen with some of the family for twenty years and have made more than a score of skiing trips to the Alps. We have also visited ski centers in Iceland, Africa, South America, Australia, and New Zealand.

When our daughter Linda was a debutante in 1947 we offered her the choice of a ski party for her friends or a ball in the grand tradition. She chose the ski party and a great one it was. We hired the big inn at Waterville Valley that had fallen on hard times and gone out of business. We assembled from all over the country a Bavarian song and dance troupe that had played at a *bierstube* in Boston until the war made German music unpopular. We provided Tyrolean costumes for all the guests and decorated the inn with an Alpine motif. It was almost empty of furniture but the Tyrolean lederhosen and dirndl skirts were suitable for sitting on the floor. The enthusiasm of the troupe proved contagious. They hadn't played together nor seen one another for half-a-dozen years and it was a great lark for them. Beer and only beer flowed freely, and even after a long day on the ski slopes dancing continued without letup for most of the night. The guests took home their Tyrolean costumes and beer mugs made especially for the occasion and I feel sure they will remember that weekend with more pleasure than any ball which might have cost five times as much.

Skiing has contributed to interesting and important friendships for our family. I came to know Averell Harriman at Sun Valley when he gave me a tongue lashing one morning for skiing too fast and then at lunch came by to apologize. This led to a discussion of the attempt by Harold Ickes, then Secretary of the Interior, to take the National Forests into his department. Later we both met in Washington appearing before a congressional committee to defeat the measure. And in the Korean War we met daily at staff meetings in the State Department and White House.

Skiing

We started skiing with Bob McNamara at Aspen before he went to Washington as Secretary of Defense and we have skied together with him and his family in every year since then. The Kennedy brothers we met at Harvard and in Boston, but we really came to know them at Aspen. I helped Prince Bernhardt when he broke his leg on Mount Tremblant (and I pulled the queen out of a snow bank). And I have hauled Lowell Thomas down the Taft Trail with a twisted knee and raced with tycoons, movie stars, and even a king. It is a humbling sport and perhaps they needed humbling as much as I.

The best of all our family trips together was a summer in Europe in 1936. We took our four children, then aged seven to fourteen, and our niece Nancy, age seventeen. Skiing and hiking rather than sightseeing was our purpose, but we had many memorable good times. We went by steamer to Le Havre and took with us a nine-passenger Dodge car equipped with heavy springs and a large rack for baggage. After skiing on the glaciers and summer snowfields of Stelvio and Obergurgl, we kayaked down some of the rapid rivers of the Alps, hiked through some of the high valleys, and climbed some of the minor peaks. Nancy and young Linda followed by automobile on our longer trips and usually met us each night stopping at tiny inns in the Alpine villages. Throughout the summer, we dressed in Tyrolean costumes and were often taken for an Austrian family. On our hike through the beautiful Karwendeltal, we never reached a road for three days. The huge waves in such glacial streams of Austria as the Inn, Salzach, and Enns, kept us wet while kayaking and would have filled our boats, but for the close-fitting spray covers. Nancy and the three boys bicycled for four days in the mountains of Bavaria and the Tyrol with limited funds, because of exchange controls, and without any adult to help them cross frontiers or find accommodations. Later, I joined them for bicycle trips in Hessia and Holland. And we ended the summer with two weeks of shooting grouse on a large, private moor in Scotland.

Years later, to celebrate our golden wedding, the children gave a party for us at Gateways and kept us in stitches acting skits based on episodes of those and other trips.

It is hard to estimate what my enthusiasm for skiing may have contributed to the advance of the sport. Certainly the number of Americans who ski has increased more than a thousand-fold since I was first introduced to the sport in 1902. For our family, skiing has been a great boon providing invaluable winter exercise, recreation, and fun.

CHAPTER XIII

⟨∞⟩

First Aid

OFTEN my own first aid training has been useful on hills and sea and may have even saved some lives. Several times have I pulled occupants from overturned or crushed automobiles and rescued skiers and hikers with broken bones. It helped when Virginia broke her leg on Butter Island. She and I were cruising on *Avelinda* in Penobscot Bay with four small granddaughters, none over eleven. We landed on the uninhabited island which we have owned since 1940. While the children played on the beach, we pushed into the dense spruce and alder woods prospecting a route for a path across to an old cellar hole and cemetery. We had gone nearly half a mile when she fell and the leg snapped. It was obviously a tibia broken near the distal end with a bad posterior dislocation of the tarsus, and it must have been very painful. I rushed back to the beach breaking off spruce twigs to mark the way lest Virginia lose consciousness from trauma and be hard to find. The children were quickly organized, the oldest sent to *Avelinda* for oaken sail battens to use as splints and bed sheets for bandages, the others to help make a trail of sorts through the thickets. When we all reached Virginia we got her leg immobilized with splints, loaded her onto my shoulders pick-a-back, and with the children ahead holding branches aside, I carried her to the beach and waded out to where they held the tender for us. With their help, we laid her in it and soon had her on a mattress on the deck of the vessel headed for Southwest Harbor. There were nearer ports, but only at Southwest had I a sister-in-law,

[131]

Linda Perkins, where I could leave the children, and a mooring where I could leave *Avelinda*. The Coast Guard was notified by radio to meet us with an ambulance, and we took her to the hospital in Bangor.

Again, I was able to help when skiing on the Parsenn above Davos. I came upon an Englishman with a compound fracture of the lower leg and a severed artery. His female companion had sent someone for the ski patrol, but the wound was bleeding profusely and he was unlikely to last until it arrived. With her help, I improvised a tourniquet, broke up a ski pole to splint the leg, and tore up a shirt for a bandage. When we finally got him by toboggan to the hospital in Klosters, the medic on triage duty immediately applied a haemostat and started a blood transfusion, while waiting for the surgeon and anesthetist to get ready to reduce the fracture.

Another close call was when helping a skier with a twisted knee on Mount Mansfield in Vermont. It was a below-zero morning, and a group of teenagers had brought a toboggan to the young chap before I arrived, but were hesitating to move him onto it because he screamed so with pain whenever they touched him. He was white with trauma and obviously would soon freeze. I got the toboggan loaded, hurried it down to the base camp, lifted it without unloading onto the table nearest the open fire in the lunch room, and there awaited a heated ambulance.

Once again, on a drag hunt with the Millwood hounds in Framingham, a young girl mounted on an excitable thoroughbred was just ahead of me as we cleared a stone wall into an orchard. Her horse swerved under the large branch of an apple tree which pulled her from the saddle and left her hanging limp and unconscious by the neck from a crotch with her feet above the ground. Instinctively I rushed to lift her down, but a yell from Doctor Wolbach who was riding ahead told me to leave her until we could organize a group to hold her head. He said we must hold it in place while lifting lest we damage the spinal cord. When

An early "skimobile" at the Laurentian Lodge Club in 1924.

The first ski ascent of Mount Katahdin in 1927.

Skiing in Vermont with my daughter Linda, 1943.

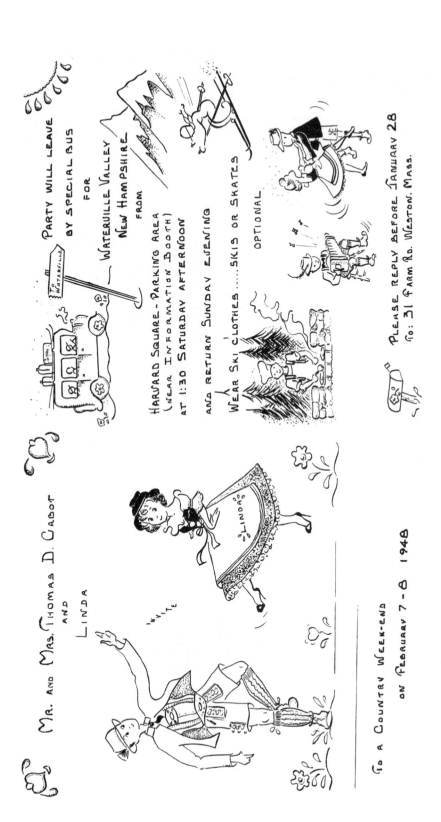

Invitation to debutante party for our daughter Linda.

Linda responding to a toast at her debutante party.

The enthusiasm of the orchestra proved contagious. Left to right (guests only): Alfred Thomas, T.D.C., Linda Perkins, Arthur Eldredge, John Mattern, Tom Zinsser.

Virginia and I at Waterville Valley party for Linda.

On our hike through the beautiful Karwendelthal region of the northern Tyrol.

We spent most of the summer of 1936 dressed in native Austrian costume exploring the eastern Alps afoot, by faltboat, ski, and bicycle. Here we are about to go down the Inn River from Innsbruck to Passau.

Nancy Wellington and our three sons bicycle in Bavaria and the Tyrol without any adult help, August 1936. Left to right: Nancy 17, Rob 12, Tommie 13, and Louis 15.

Linda Cabot and Pussy Endicott bring lunch to the hunters shooting grouse on the Glenspaen moor in Scotland, September 1936.

she was carefully spread on the ground, she appeared to be dead, but Wolbach took the pin from his stock to prick her leg and knew from her flinch that the cord was not severed. She regained consciousness before the ambulance arrived and the hospital found her major injury to be only a badly broken jaw.

Fortunately when accidents have happened to me and to others in the family, first aid has been readily available. The only exception was the recent loss of my right eye. My eyes had survived the terrors of the age of hat pins and the threats from flying chips through years of work with the axe, but now while passing through a hemlock grove in deep snow, I reached out a hand to break a brittle twig, a small piece flew back and destroyed the eye. Only with great difficulty could I make my way to where I could get help. Moral: always wear protective glasses when walking or working in the woods. And the same advice should apply for fly-fishing and working with tools.

CHAPTER XIV

◌◌◌◌

Hunting and Ranching

TWO years after our marriage, when we moved back from West Virginia to our new home in Weston, we brought our horses with us. Before this town was transformed from a farming community to a dormitory suburb of Boston, we had a network of bridle trails, could ride through woods and fields in every direction, and enjoyed riding almost every day. We soon took up fox hunting with the various hunt clubs, and also drag hunting by laying an artificial scent for the hounds to follow. Our own club was Millwood in Framingham, but we also rode with the Dedham and Norfolk clubs, and once or twice with the Groton Hunt. We could reach these hunts on horseback along trails and country roads. By World War II, much of the hunting country was spoiled by real estate development and paved highways, so we had to get a trailer to transport our horses to the more distant country of the Myopia and Quonsett hunts.

In the 1930's we made a number of riding trips in Vermont on hired horses. On these excursions we were usually accompanied by friends and stayed at small inns, leaving our horses in the barns of the inn or at nearby farms. After the war, farms and inns no longer had horse barns and we began to do much of our riding in New Hampshire using a trailer to transport our horses there behind an automobile. Moving them back and forth from Massachusetts each weekend was a chore, so we bought a chalet in the woods of Sharon, New Hampshire. Nowadays we keep our horses and trailer at a stable not far from Sharon and pick them up on our way to the chalet, leaving them on the way home.

From our chalet, there must be 2,000 miles of trails within a radius of twenty miles. That country was once heavily farmed, but with the advent of the railroads that brought grain from the Middle West, the New England farms were gradually abandoned along with many of the roads. These "lost" roads provide interesting rides, and we are still exploring new trails even after more than a decade of covering the neighborhood.

We no longer hunt, but before we gave it up we had some delightful ones in different parts of the world. We have hunted with some of the famous packs of Maryland, Virginia, and North Carolina and with several packs in England.

On my first visit to England after World War II, friends with whom I had hunted in Sussex suggested that I must have a hunt in Ireland before I returned home. They borrowed a horse for me and arranged a hunt with the United Club near Cork. I arrived to find the country flooded. At a cocktail party that evening, it was predicted that there would be no chance to hunt for at least a week. Someone suggested that the Duhallow pack would be hunting next day in the high country to the north, and that Dick Sheehan could job me a horse. I knew of Sheehan through mutual friends and telephoned him, but all my pleading came to naught. It was too far from his stable to the meet, and he had no petrol to box a horse thither. I thought I would let drop a few names that might influence him; it didn't, but as I was about to hang up he asked me my name, and on discovering that I was the cousin of the founder of the State Street Mutual Fund, in which he had a profitable investment, I suddenly found that I was a hero not to be denied. He immediately undertook to have the meet moved to Steeple Hill, near his stable, and to job me "the best hunter in all Ireland." It is Steeple Hill for which the steeplechase is named.

He certainly had a superb horse ready for me next morning. It won a blue ribbon at Dublin that year, and I needed such a horse for the huge Irish banks for which the Steeple Hill country is famous. There never was such a ride. Before we started, Sheehan told me to put politeness aside and disregard the "West Britons" (English) and follow either O'Mara, who was on another magnificent thoroughbred, or the padre, who was acting as whipper-in, dressed in top hat, black frock coat, reversed collar, well-pegged black breeches, and well-polished boots. I won't mention the name of the priest—he even refused to have his picture taken in such a regalia lest it fall into the hands of the bishop. We hunted all day and drove three foxes to earth. By mid-afternoon the field started back for the stables, but suddenly the pack gave tongue. They dashed through a copse to the opposite side of the valley in full cry with the fox in sight ahead. We took off hell-for-leather disregarding all thoughts of protocol. The less well-mounted MFH struggled to keep up. I found myself abreast of O'Mara with no one ahead.

Irish banks are actually stone walls with drainage ditches on both sides. The clay soil from the ditches is piled against the wall. It is a good twelve feet from the edge of the near ditch to the top of the wall beyond and another twelve feet to the far edge of the ditch on the other side. No animal could fly the bank and both ditches in a single jump, but these Irish hunters are trained to jump to the top of the wall, which they touch with all four hooves, getting a spring with their hind legs to clear the further ditch. The tops of the walls are but a few inches wide and are often more than five feet higher than the field on either side, so there is no possibility of seeing what lies beyond. I had no knowledge of the country and didn't notice when O'Mara beside me swerved right at a high wall. When the horse and I came over the top there was a hidden boreen, like a sunken road, deep below me. We were traveling fast and couldn't stop. The horse and I must have fallen nearly ten feet into the mud of the road. I remember throwing myself so that my shoulder would hit the neck of the horse, and the next thing I knew I was lying in the mud with my wind knocked out and O'Mara above me shouting, "Get up, the fox is running!" He helped me into the saddle and away we went again, this time with him in the lead.

Some time later at another high bank which he had led by some yards, I came over the top to see him in a slough beyond with his horse almost totally immersed. In a second I was beside him wallowing in the muddy pond. We pulled the horses out by their bridles. Cold, wet, and completely smeared with mud, we decided it was time to find a public house.

That was my most memorable hunt but my wife and I have had a number of others which we remember fondly. Stag hunts in the forests of Normandy have been especially pleasant for us; they are quite different from English fox hunts. There is more pageantry and attention to the working of the hounds, but far less jumping or fast riding.

The privilege of stag hunting in Foret d'Andane and in Foret d'Ecove is leased annually from the national government by Equipage Kermaingant. The hunting is for Saturdays only and for a limited number of stags (*cerfs*) each year. Other hunting groups on other days of the week have permits to hunt the roebuck (*chevreuil*) or the wild boar (*sanglier*). These national forests are of limited area—perhaps fifty square miles—and they are surrounded by farmland. The deer rarely leave the forested area. Silviculture is more intensive in France than here. There is little undergrowth and low branches are relatively few, so that one can ride at a good pace through the trees. Actually, most of the riding is on trails or wood roads used for harvesting the timber. If one gallops off the trail, there is danger of falling into a fox hole or shell crater left from the war. We rarely gallop and skilled horsemanship is hardly necessary.

On a typical stag hunt weekend, we would leave Paris with friends on a Friday afternoon and be entertained at one or another of the great chateaux in western Normandy. In the morning, with a couple of younger friends, I am invited to rise at five, dress in old clothes, and explore the forest afoot, each with one hound on a leash. There we look for the largest of the fresh stag tracks. Returning to the chateau by 9:00, we dress in the magnificent hunting costumes of Equipage Kermaingant, long scarlet hunting coats with yellow collars and black piping, white breeches, and stiff black boots above the knee in front. We sit down to a hunt breakfast where Monsieur Kermaingant listens to advice as to which *piste* to follow. After breakfast the whole party, including much of the local gentry and others who have arrived from Paris, mount the sleek thoroughbred horses for which Normandy is famous, and ride to the forest.

On arrival at the prearranged rendezvous, we find a large pack of hounds in the charge of a huntsman. Besides the fancy costumes worn by members of the hunt of both sexes, all of the male members are equipped with a small sword carried in a silver scabbard attached to a Sam Browne belt of gold braid. Also each man has a large French hunting horn of brass coiled over the right shoulder and under the left arm which is used for communication and a long whip of braided leather for managing the hounds. When all is ready, a small group of hounds is released near the *piste* that was selected from those found in the early morning. The scent is now several hours old, and the hounds follow it in a rather lackadaisical manner until they come to the point where the stag has lain down for his noon siesta. There the hounds give tongue and start to dash off in pursuit, but the nearest hunter bugles the *arrêt* and all riders attempt to hold the hounds in check until the rest of the large pack has been brought up to join the chase. Another bugle call starts the whole pack in full cry on the hot trail. The riders disperse to follow the progress of the chase as best they can. They do not follow behind the hounds, for that would be impossible through the woods, but one can hear the yelps of the pack from a mile away, and the secret of keeping in touch is to anticipate which way the stag will turn.

An old but inexperienced American, who can't recognize one bugle call from another, will naturally have picked the prettiest girl as his guide. We trot off in the direction she recommends. Soon there are diverse tunes from the many horns dispersed throughout the forest, each telling the story of the chase: whether the hounds are closing on the stag, which way the stag is heading, and other such news to help members of the hunt anticipate the course of the chase, give them a view of the running animal and eager hounds, and enable them to be close at hand when the stag is finally brought to bay. The hunt lasts several hours.

Once we took seven hours to bring to bay a mighty stag. Obviously no horse can gallop so long, and actually there is little need to hurry except when the bugle calls that the faltering stag has turned at bay. Then everyone rushes to be in at the finish. It is most important that a man with a sword be close by when this happens, and he must boldly rush in through the circle of yapping hounds and quickly stab the animal through the neck into the heart before it has a chance to recover its breath and become dangerous. If ready to fight, a 400-pound stag could easily disembowel a man with a single blow of its sharp cloven hoof.

On a short winter day it is usually approaching dusk before the chase is over. The local farmers who have been following the hunt by ear will drag the dead stag to the nearest farmyard where it is butchered. The best meat is then distributed among the neighbors and the remainder left for the hounds. The left forehoof is presented to one of the ladies as a token of honor. While all this is going on the *cureé* begins. A bonfire is built and the party gathers around. Sandwiches and flasks of brandy appear and a few of the better buglers stand on one side of the fire and the remainder on the other. The bugles calling back and forth across the flaming embers tell the whole story of the hunt. The hounds stand by with dripping jaws and are not allowed their share of the meat until the *cureé* is over. They know that at the last note of the bugle announcing the kill, the hide of the stag will be thrown off from their share of the meat and they will be allowed quickly to devour their reward, which is the first meal they have had in a long day.

Such fox or stag hunting with horses is an anachronism and some may think it cruel. I don't want to argue the point. I was never a great admirer of collections of wild game prepared by taxidermists to adorn the walls of living room or den. The hunting instinct is strong in a man. The joy one derives from the hunt is proportional to the difficulty of the success and not to the quantity of meat. Riding to hounds is a sport that bears only a marginal relationship to killing animals, whether they be fox or stag. Most of our riding to hounds has been at drag hunts. Here the quarry is only a scented bag which makes it an even more artificial sport. In fact, it is so artificial that I wonder why we trouble to have a pack of hounds to follow. As our hunting country in New England fills up with real estate development, paved highways, and fences, it becomes unsuitable for jumping. With the spread of suburbia and the abandonment of farms it has become almost impossible to hunt fox. Even on a prepared course the drag hunt is difficult.

A different kind of hunting in which we sometimes use horses but more often jeeps is hunting the deer and elk in the Rocky Mountains. Occasionally, I used to hunt deer in the East, and I have very much enjoyed the house parties of the Carnegie family at Cumberland Island in Georgia and of the Forbes family at Naushon Island in Massachusetts. On both of these islands the herds of deer are too large for the supply of browse and hunting is needed to hold down the deer population. Now, in recent years, we hunt only in the West on a ranch which our company leases in Colorado high in the Sangre de Christo Mountains.

We acquired this ranch, Bar NI, by lease from CF&I Steel Corporation during World War II. At that time we were having difficulty keeping our personnel at the company's operating headquarters in Pampa, Texas, and at the plants thereabouts. This was particularly true of engineers who were recruited from the East. Our chief engineer conceived the idea that if we could offer our staff a place where they could fish on weekends they might

Introducing Ned to the Milwood Hunt Club at a drag hunt in Framingham in 1949.

Linda provides wartime transportation for the residents of Hidden Hearth without the use of gasoline.

Deer hunt on Naushon Island, 1941. Left to right: Nancy Hosmer, Cam Forbes, Virginia Cabot, Sra. de Cordemas, Marnie Schroeder, Eliz. Clark, Mary Rentschler, Charlie Coolidge, Harold Keith, Henry Hosmer, Mary Colt, Eric Schroeder, Wendell Endicott, Copley Amory, Alison Coolidge, Copley Amory, Jr., Gordon Rentschler.

Home again at War's end, December 1945. Left to right: Virginia, Ned, Lieut. T.D.C., Jr., Linda, Sgt. R.M.C., Lieut. L.W.C., Mary Lou, and T.D.C., Sr.

Ready to ride at our Bar NI Ranch in the Sangre de Christo Mountains of Colorado.

Entrance to Bar NI Ranch at Stonewall, Colorado leased by Cabot Corporation for the benefit of its employees in the Southwest and for guests in the elk hunting season.

be happier. Our lease covers the fishing, hunting, and camping on nearly fifty thousand acres. These were available for a nominal rental in consideration for our agreeing to fix up a lodge that was formerly a headquarters for cattle operations, but had been vacant for a dozen years and was badly vandalized. The renovated lodge is now made available to salaried personnel at a small charge. Smaller cottages as well as camping privileges are offered free to all employees and their families. The main attraction is the fishing in the several trout brooks. We estimate that about 10,000 trout are taken per year, an equivalent number of fingerlings being added to those which spawn in the streams and ponds.

I never saw the ranch during the war, but after Thanksgiving in 1945 I stopped there with our son Rob, who had just returned from three years of fighting in Europe. We were en route to meet the rest of the family at the wedding of our oldest son Louis in California. Although both of us had done a lot of riding and camping in the West, we were naturally thought of as Eastern dudes by the Texans whom we met at the ranch. They took us on a horseback trip up into the snow where we got lost and waded through drifts until after dark, getting back to the lodge not long before midnight. Tall Texas tales passed freely, and when they got onto the subject of our neighbors in those wild hills, they said that the ranch to the south was as large as Rhode Island and completely surrounded by a high fence with locked gates through which no one was permitted to pass without a written permit, and that anyone caught inside the fence was shot on sight. They then went on to tell about the ranch house itself, saying it had sixty-five bedrooms and was built at the turn of the century at a cost of several million dollars. Nothing daunted, we wanted to visit the property and scoffed at their tales of prohibited entry. After two days of taunting them and appealing to their Texas manhood we finally persuaded them to take us there by motor. The property was known as Vermejo Park and was aquired by the Bartlett family as a summer home until the founder died in 1911. The ranch was then sold to a Los Angeles syndicate headed by Mr. Chandler of the *Times Mirror* who operated it as a club and leased the grazing rights to a Mr. Ayton.

On the way to the ranch gate, we stopped for gasoline and were again told that under no circumstances should we go on the property without written permission. The gate was a massive iron structure on pintles with a heavy chain and padlock, but it didn't take us long to lift it off the pintles and get inside. We met no one on the twenty-eight-mile driveway. The ranch house was an enormous tile-roofed, stucco structure with two wings and a porte cochere between the central structure and each wing. As we approached it we could see in the windows people in formal evening clothes. One of the women came out onto the porch and stared at us. She beckoned us toward the porte cochere. A huge man in a silk shirt, frontier breeches, and high-heeled cowboy boots met us with arms held akimbo, showing off his biceps. Our Texas driver started to stammer apologies, while I came around the car and held out my hand to introduce myself as a friend of Mr. Chandler's. There was a painful pause while his arms stayed akimbo. Finally, as I withdrew my hand, this man, whom I later recognized as Ayton, said, with no change in his expression, "Mr. Chandler passed away three years ago. He permitted no visitors, the order still stands." With apologies, I returned to the car. We backed out of the porte cochere and went back the twenty-eight miles to the gate, which we again removed from the pintles to leave the property.

A few months later, the property was sold to an oil man named Gourley from Fort Worth, who took over the cattle business and operated the ranch house as a public hunting lodge until the central building burned ten years later. The two wings still stand as magnificent structures and are used largely by wealthy Texans who come there to fish and to hunt. There is another fine lodge on part of the property that also takes in paying guests. We have been on more friendly terms with the recent owners and have made several delightful pack trips with horses on parts of the property.

It didn't take long for our son Rob to persuade his mother that she would enjoy being hostess at our ranch, and, until my retirement, we usually spent about a month or six weeks there each summer during which time we would take one or more camping trips. The Sangre de Christo are beautiful mountains. The view from the lodge is of the Spanish Peaks. The ranch headquarters is at 8,100 feet of altitude and the back of the property is more than 13,000 feet. All of our children and most of our grandchildren have accompanied us on pack trips with horses in those mountains. The country is still very wild and beautiful, and we have explored the range from 120 miles north of the ranch to sixty miles south. There is only one public road crossing the mountains in all that distance.

At first, we did no hunting, but enjoyed looking at the deer, elk, turkeys, bear, cougar, and coyotes. However, on one business trip to Akron, at a luncheon with an important customer, he told me of the enjoyable trip he had had with one of our competitors at their large property in the Ozarks. I told him I felt sure we could do better, and invited him to visit us at our ranch during the elk hunting season. Other friends were invited to join us and this became an annual affair. Now, there are usually at least two elk hunting parties at the ranch each fall. At each about a score of hunters from among the executives of companies with whom we do business spend several days exploring the ranch by jeep or horseback. As honorary chairman, I am still permitted to act as a "guide."

The major use of the ranch continues to be the accommodation of employees from our Pampa office and from our plants and oil operations in the Southwest. They come with families and it is a great satisfaction to have many letters each fall telling me how much the ranch privileges are appreciated. Although a majority of the employees who use the ranch like to camp out at idyllic spots in the valleys, very few explore the high peaks above timber line. The members of my family, all of whom are good riders, enjoy this remote timber line country the most. It used to be possible to reach the high slopes only by pushing through the woods on game trails, but now there are dozed roads built to get out logs. The roads are a boon to hunters, for without them it would be difficult to bring the meat back to the lodge. A bull elk weighs up to 1,500 pounds, and even a deer is not easily packed on the back of a horse.

We have enjoyed the ranch for more than thirty years, and would enjoy it more if our tenure were secure, but our landlord is not inclined to sell. Virginia and I have built many bridle trails for our guests and have worked to improve the views from the lodge and other vantage points. We dread the possibility that our family and friends may be deprived of this property which has meant so much to all of us for so many years.

CHAPTER XV

⌒∾⌒

Love of Unspoiled Islands

ISLAND adventures such as happened to Robinson Crusoe have always fascinated me. I never thought about owning an island until after we had children. On one of our early cruises by chartered yacht, we anchored one stormy night in a wild cove within one of the smaller archipelagoes of Penobscot Bay. The chartered vessel was a small one, and one of our boys had to sleep on deck. The lot fell to the eight-year-old. He was sleeping next to the toerail on an air mattress in a mummy-like sleeping bag. After midnight, I heard splashing. When I rushed on deck, in the dim starlight I saw a shape drifting astern with the tide. I dived off the side and with a few strokes came onto the floating bag, but there was no boy inside. He had only recently learned to swim and I feared the worst, but presently there was an answering call to my shouts coming from the bow of the vessel, and I found that the youngster had swum to the bobstay and was holding on there. He had no way to climb aboard. The others were aroused and helped us to the deck. We put the shivering youngster into my warm bed, which left me only a cold seat on deck. As dawn came, I reflected on the possibility of buying that wild archipelago that showed no signs of ownership. An investigation led me to a man named Smith in Chelsea. He told me he had bought the property for almost nothing at the suggestion of a cousin who lived on an island not far away, but that his feeling was that he should offer the property to a member of his family before dealing with an outsider. Frustrated in this attempt,

I began looking up the ownership of other nearby islands and found one for sale but the price was much higher than I could afford. Years passed and when the owner died my interest became known to the heirs. The island was offered to me at a reasonable price, and I bought it. That was at the beginning of World War II, and, after Pearl Harbor, I was offered other islands. In those days a small island in Maine would sell for $100 or even less, and I soon had quite a collection, including such large ones as Cross Island and Butter Island.

It was fun buying this real estate to preserve its primeval beauty. I have watched the prices at which islands are sold escalate a hundred-fold but have not been tempted to sell. The taxes have risen even more, which may jeopardize the future of these unspoiled shores. The purchases I made were from local people who were eager to sell. Generally I learned of these from conversations with lobstermen.

Now when we cruise the coast of Maine, we enjoy stopping at our islands and exploring the woods. We get a lot of enjoyment from ownership, but we do have the usual problems with litter and vandalism. We have some hundreds of small aluminum tags posted along the shores each bearing the notation: AVE-LINDA FOREST – The Owner Asks You to Help Protect the Beauty of This Area – NO FIRES, NO SMOKE, NO LITTER, NO DAMAGE TO TREES AND SHRUBS. The number of people who land to picnic and camp is growing exponentially. Fortunately the public seems to be learning to respect the woods and shores. Despite the larger crowds, there are fewer instances of deliberate vandalism and there is less accumulation of litter. Policing is difficult as no one lives on the properties.

Last summer a young man, who might be characterized as a hobo, started to build a stone cabin on one of my islands. He built it deep in the woods, obscuring the entry trail by crawling under spruce boughs. The sound of an axe and the smell of wood smoke betrayed him. When discovered, he carried a pistol which he fingered ominously. Police authority was no help in getting him to move off. Ultimately, after several visits to his camp, he was persuaded to leave by notes left on his bed threatening court action.

We bought Cross Island through a squatter who fished the nearby waters. He told me that, after a paper company had harvested the pulp wood on the island, the property was sold to a Maine guide who intended to bring sportsmen from Boston to hunt deer there out of season. With the advent of war, the guide found it difficult to attract sportsmen and wished to sell. I made an offer to buy the island and nearby islets at his cost which was accepted. That was in February 1942, and over the three-day holiday weekend of April 19th, I went with my son Tom, to visit the island. We went by night train to Machias, carrying a German folding kayak as baggage. It had a swastika emblem on it, and when we started to set up the kayak on the bank of the Machias River the police came and wanted to check our credentials. My son was an officer of the Navy on active duty, and I had a Coast Guard identification, but it took some time to convince the gathering crowd that we weren't spies. At that time the Coast Guard had about forty men stationed on the island to protect it from the Germans. We had notified them in advance of our arrival. It was snowing hard, and as we left the river to paddle down the bay, the outgoing tide against the strong southeast wind had built up an awesome rip. We were really in no danger, but when the Coast Guard picket boat came to meet us we had great difficulty persuading the crew to let us go on rather than risk overturning in an attempt to tow us or take us aboard.

We arrived safely at a beach in the lee of Cross Island and found a deserted shack. Soon we had a fire going to dry out our clothes and restore some body heat. Raw recruits of the Coast Guard were patrolling the island in pairs and next morning when we were exploring the island we were stopped innumerable times. In each case we were greeted with orders to hold up our hands, and while they kept us covered with cocked pistols, we were ordered separately to place our credentials on the ground and back away for the papers to be examined. I shudder to think what would have happened had one of those nervous youngsters with shaking fingers fired an accidental shot.

It took us twelve hours to walk around the shore of the whole island. We stopped to talk to the two squatters. They were brothers who lived on opposite sides of the property and carried on a feud over the boundaries within which each might set out lobster traps. To each of them we insisted that there should be no more feuding, that we would allow them to continue to occupy their cabins and act as caretakers, and that we would charge $1.00 a year as rent, thus avoiding the question of squatter's rights. Both of the brothers continued to live on the island until they died, and we became good friends. There was no more feuding between them and each took good care of his part of the island.

On our trip around the island we had a good chance to admire the fine cliffs of the outer shore and to visit a cave which at low tide one can enter for a distance of over a hundred feet. We also saw the water-filled hole left by a copper mining operation of a hundred years earlier. There were many sheep pastured on the island owned by a former sea captain from Buck's Harbor who let them run wild until shearing time. The island had formerly been occupied by a good many families. There had even been a store carrying ship chandlery and groceries for sale to the coasting vessels that would anchor in the narrows during bad weather. On the eastern end of the island was an abandoned lifesaving station still in good repair to which we had acquired title. This was built in 1874 when rescue operations were conducted by surf boats launched from a ramp and rowed to sea. Later, when the surf boats were replaced by larger diesel powered rescue boats, the Coast Guard moved into a larger frame building with marine railway that faces the sheltered water where boats can be moored throughout the year. These newer buildings were built in 1917 on a five-acre lot taken by condemnation from a former owner of the island.

The Coast Guard continued its operations on the island for a number of years after the war, and we enjoyed the friendship of the personnel stationed there. One evening two of these friends came aboard *Avelinda* for cocktails. It was quite cool when they left, and the next morning we learned they were found in their berths on a picket boat at its mooring near us, dead from carbon monoxide poisoning. At a hearing, I was asked to testify that they were not intoxicated when they left us, but this was hardly necessary because others testified that they had played several games of pool after leaving us. Since this experience, I've always been afraid of coal stoves in a closed cabin.

When the Coast Guard operation was abandoned in the 1950's I tried to buy the five-acre reservation and buildings. For several years there were conflicting reports as to why the government couldn't consider an offer, and I finally realized it must be due to a flaw in the title. I found that there were several cases in other states where owners of land taken by eminent domain for a specific purpose successfully claimed reversion after termination of the purpose. With this knowledge I managed to find a lawyer in the General Services Administration who would consider an offer based on the government's right only to recover the movables on the property, and my modest offer for these movables was quickly accepted.

At about that time, the Hurricane Island Outward Bound School, in which I had become quite interested, was having difficulty in negotiating a renewal lease to its base on Hurricane Island. Wanting to provide the school with an alternative as a sort of anchor to windward, I gave them a deed to these Cross Island buildings and equipment and to a somewhat larger acreage. Also, I gave a ten-year lease free of rental on the rest of the island and nearby islets. Excluded from the lease was a part of the western point which I had previously sold to a lobsterman in Cutler who had lost his property by condemnation.

On this first visit after our purchase, my son and I also crossed the narrows to the mainland at Thornton Point where we had heard chainsaws at work. We found the cutting of pulp wood there was nearly completed. The company that had bought the land to cut it was willing to sell the end of the point, including about a mile and a half of shorefront, at $1.00 an acre after removal of the pulp wood. I offered double the asking price if they would leave the remaining trees. We settled at that price.

Some years later the Navy wanted this mainland property for a radio station. An offer to let the government have it free of charge if it would leave the fringe of trees was refused. We subsequently agreed on a price but the Navy wouldn't accept a quitclaim deed, and I refused to give a general warranty because of possible flaws in the title. This forced the Navy to condemn the property with the price stipulated. Years after I had received my money, I was notified by the Federal District Court that I had received it illegally. Although the Navy was satisfied, the court had discovered that the stipulation I had signed had not been signed by a claimant to a small lot included in the property. The court threatened me with judgments and even incarceration, and it took nearly two years of correspondence and conferences to cut through the red tape and get the federal attorney to absolve me. Now this radio station, with its twenty-five 900-foot towers, is the most conspicuous landmark on the eastern coast.

My ownership of Cross Island led to a day in court, where I was a leading witness. In the early 1970's, Occidental Petroleum Company wanted to build a refinery on Machias Bay, and I joined with other conservationists in opposing it. The proposal was to create a free port sponsored by the state which would condemn enough land to cover the needs of the refinery and ancillary industries, as well as a 1,500-foot dock on the exposed side of Stone Island. My opposition was due not just to the impairment of the

scenic beauty of that part of the coast, but also because the proposal was grossly unfair to other processors of crude oil and semi-
refined products, including Cabot Corporation. At that time, oil
imports were restricted by quota, and Occidental was asking for
such a disproportionate quota that it would have profited about
one-hundred percent per year on its investment from the quota
alone.

The hearing was in the Court House at Portland, and the place
was crowded, with many unable to gain admittance. I recognized
in the crowd many representatives of the oil companies, and several suggested that I be the first witness. However, Hale Boggs,
the Congressman from Louisiana, was there and I gave way to
him. Louis Nizer, the famous trial lawyer from New York rep-
resented Occidental. On the bench were representatives of the
three federal departments concerned: Treasury, Commerce, and
Army. Boggs felt that he had been offered bribes to stay away,
and put on a magnificent display of righteousness. From then on
it was easy to show up the iniquity of the proposal, and I took
delight in posing as an expert in the various fields of ecology,
navigation, and oil economics. The application was denied.

I have mentioned the two brothers who squatted on Cross
Island and feuded with each other. Their reputations along the
coast were far from exemplary, and there is little doubt that they
lived in self-imposed exile as hermits. They had plenty of chances
to take advantage of me, but I came to feel them trustworthy
with respect to liquid assets, unless contained in a bottle. They
taught me a lot about the perils of the sea and about the early
glories of that part of the coast. Their grandfather had mined
copper on Double Shot Island and had fought in the Civil War.
At their urging we landed on the Double Shot Islands and on
Old Man Island, both of which we now own. The abandoned
mine on the headland of outer Double Shot is quite impressive,
and landing on Old Man is also a memorable experience. These
are both outer islands, and there is no easy landing point on either,

so they can be visited only in very calm weather. Both have large rookeries of sea birds. The number of gulls and cormorants nesting on Old Man Island is greater than at any other point on the coast.

To fortify the American position in discussions with Denmark over salmon fisheries, the United States government needed more information on the habits of the anadromous Atlantic salmon. Accordingly, a program was started of stapling inch-long nylon tapes to the dorsal fin of fingerling parr in the Machias River. Each tape bears a number and a $1.00 offer to anyone returning the tape with information as to the location where the fish is taken. The office was getting few tapes returned until one day a Maine fisherman brought in a whole bucketful. After making sure that they would pay him $1.00 each, he revealed that he had collected them on Old Man Island. Imagine how much guano he must have sifted to earn the reward.

Because so many of the salmon raised at federal hatcheries are being eaten by shore birds on the way to sea, the federal government has been destroying eggs in this great rookery—an expensive and hazardous job on such formidable cliffs. Now, the state of Maine, in an attempt to save eider ducks, has declared the Old Man a critical area and asked me to stop everyone from landing there during the nesting season, an obvious impossibility. I have received more than two hundred pages of correspondence about this federal vs. state conflict, which must have cost the taxpayers more than the whole island is worth.

There was another interesting result from buying real estate further west along the coast. One foggy morning my wife and I landed the *Avelinda* on the north shore of Swans Island and walked a mile along the shore through woods that showed no sign of recent human use. We came to a fisherman's cottage where an elderly man was repairing lobster traps. We asked him about the ownership of the land, and he told us that it had been sold a few weeks before by a local ne'er-do-well for a few hundred dollars, and that a real estate man from Bar Harbor had resold it for several thousand dollars. When we expressed regret that we hadn't had a chance to put in a bid, he said that his own house was for sale and wanted to show us through it. We weren't looking for a house, but when he mentioned that there were eighty acres on Swans Island plus several islets and a part ownership of Buckle Island that went with the property, we were more interested. He quoted a price he got from a real estate man, and it seemed reasonable to us. Having no use for the house and not wanting to deprive the lobsterman of its use, we thanked him and went on our way. A day or two later at a cocktail party, Peggy Rockefeller asked me if I would sell her one of my islands. I declined, but offered to buy her one. I told her of my conversation with the lobsterman and of my intention to return to make a deal with him, but I didn't expect her to get there ahead of me. When I found she had been to see him, I feared the worst, but the lobsterman stuck to his offer, and I was able to get the property, giving him a lease-back to the house free of charge. Thus, Mrs. Rockefeller got her island, and soon began to buy a good deal of other undeveloped shorefront nearby. As prices rose, she asked my advice as to how we could save the coast, and I recommended voluntary scenic restrictions as one alternative, suggesting that this was probably the cheapest and most permanent way of preserving the primeval quality of undeveloped land. This led to her founding the Maine Coast Heritage Trust, which for me is a very pleasant association. The trust continues to be quite effective in saving many islands and headlands from unsightly development.

Voluntary restrictions are an old idea and have been used elsewhere for conservation, but they are not always more appropriate than conveying the fee title to the land itself to either a conservation organization or to a public agency. The important advantage of a conservation restriction over other alternatives is that, with the owner retaining fee title to the land, he also retains the privacy of its use. No rights are provided for public access unless the owner grants specific permission. By continuing to pay taxes on the value which he has limited by the restrictions, he continues to enjoy his property in privacy as he chooses, consistent with the terms of the restriction. He may continue to live on it or to use it for agriculture or silviculture, provided it is kept in a natural scenic or open condition. The public continues to benefit from taxes on the land, but not on development which would, in the long run, increase the costs of government more than the additional taxes.

My interest in the subject had led to a study of the whole matter of land use and how one can plan and control it. The ecology of Maine islands, especially the small ones, is very fragile. I doubt that it would be a service to posterity to create public parks of these islands. For this reason, I have preferred to protect my own islands by scenic easements which limit development rather than give them to an agency that may not deny public access.

My interest is not only in Maine, but also helping conservation organizations in New Hampshire and Massachusetts. In 1975 the Trustees of Reservations of Massachusetts named me "Conservationist of the Year," and I was asked to speak on land use. Since than I have attended and spoken at several conferences on the subject. I don't feel that conservation is the most important of my philanthropic interests, but none has given us more pleasure.

Our favorite "gunk-hole" for shelter when cruising in eastern Maine is Haycock Harbor. It has a headland to the east of its entrance with a magnificent spot of luxurious ground and splendid views. Years ago it was completely primeval, and I wanted to own it. A lobsterman told me that it was owned by a man named Hurst, but he didn't know the address. I wrote to several nearby post offices, and a reply came from the postmistress at West Trescott saying that the owner was her husband. Thinking that this would probably be a local fisherman, I wrote to him offering $500 for that exposed point, explaining that I was a yachtsman and had visited it. The letter in reply was pecked out on a typewriter with many corrections on a cheap piece of lined paper. It declined my offer, but seemed consistent with my assumption that he was a fisherman, so I wrote again, hoping I might be able to buy some small part of the property. The next letter I received suggested that I take my money to Wonderland and invest it in a bet on a greyhound, and maybe I might win enough money to make a real offer. Well, it took me nearly a year of correspondence before I realized that I was being led on by an expert of considerable background. I found myself rankled that I had no crew on my yacht, whereas he had had a yacht with five foremast hands. He also kidded me about my Harvard background and I felt sure that he had gone to Yale. When I told him that the delay in my correspondence was caused by a month-long trip to Darjeeling in the Himalayas, he told me he had been to visit Lhasa in Tibet. By then I knew that I was up against something pretty interesting. The letters continued to be on cheap school-block paper and were obviously typewritten with one finger. Determined to look him up, I found that he had moved to Calais. The following summer when Virginia and I, with some friends, sailed up the St. Croix River to Calais, we went to call on Hurst. The address was a huge house left over from the days when the lumber industry brought prosperity to Calais. It was quite run down. The elaborate oaken front door had a large hasp crudely nailed on and was locked by padlock. The house was not occupied, so we had to peek in the windows under drawn shades. It was filled with books and magazines piled ceiling high. We decided to return to the village, and needing a haircut, I went into the barbershop and started to gossip with the barber. He told me that Mr. Hurst was, "a wizened up little shrimp older than Methuselah and richer than Croesus," and that he had a "five-by-five" wife.

The next letter from Hurst said that he had moved back to

Trescott. We tried to find him there, but again the house was locked. We were told by neighbors that he and Mrs. Hurst were living deep in the woods east of Haycock Harbor and that the abandoned school bus in which they were living could be reached by following a swamped-out trail which Mrs. Hurst had personally cut with a chainsaw. President and Mrs. Pusey of Harvard were cruising with us on *Avelinda* at the time, and needing the exercise we walked through the woods along this crude jeep trail. When we reached the school bus, we found a tiny wizened old man sitting on a stump in front of it. Although it was midsummer, he was wearing a stocking cap, two heavy overcoats, galoshes, and mitts. He was stooped forward with his chin on his chest. I introduced myself and held out my hand, but as he was getting off his glove to take it, I received a heavy push on the shoulder, and Mrs. Hurst admonished me not to touch him as it would hurt him dreadfully. She certainly had the build to both push me aside and swamp-out a road.

Hurst was delighted to meet President Pusey, and we talked of the Yale connection. Hurst said he had been wanting to give money to Yale but didn't quite know where to send it, and Pusey undertook to have President Griswold of Yale write him a letter. This was the first of several talks I had with Hurst. When he died some months later I found that he had left a gold pencil for me, and I was given a small lot facing the head of Haycock Harbor. Subsequently, Mrs. Hurst told me of a very bright high school boy whom she had befriended and who wanted to be a doctor. I offered to help him through Yale, but jealousy developed between the boy's mother and Mrs. Hurst, and the scholarship I had given Yale went to another Maine lad. The first boy did succeed in getting a scholarship to a less well known university, and he is now a doctor practicing in Maine.

I wish I knew more of the history of Julius Hurst, but I can only give an outline of his life. He was the scion of a prominent textile family in Lancashire, England. While at Harrow his parents died, and an uncle who held the purse strings tried to force him into the textile business. He went to Tasmania where he scraped up enough money to come to America and entered the medical school at Yale in 1895. Before graduating, he was accused by the dean of lying about his tardy return from a vacation in Paris and was denied a degree despite his plea of innocence. After a year at another medical school he got a residency for two years in a London hospital and finally he got an M.D. degree from Yale, but not until 1904. By then he was married and was practicing medicine in Connecticut and had a large yacht. After he lost his wife he moved to California. There, while driving on a country road with a girl he had picked up as a hitchhiker, the car overturned, killing her and severely injuring him. After he got out of the hospital, he decided to go to Maine to console the girl's family. While there he fell in love with the girl's younger sister who was also many years his junior. He married her and they went to live in Santa Barbara. When war broke out in 1914, he wanted to be commissioned as a doctor in the British or Canadian Army. He was rejected by both because he was underweight. Finally he got a commission in the American Army but only through the intercession of the Surgeon General. He served in field hospitals in Flanders until the war was over.

After the war he served in the Veterans Administration until his retirement when they returned to Maine. He was badly afflicted with arthritis and was not able to hold a book or pencil, but he could peck out a letter on a typewriter. Despite his affliction, he had tremendous courage and a fine sense of humor. I don't believe he weighed more than ninety pounds when he died.

My ownership of Maine islands led to a very different venture in another part of the world. John Mecum, who owned a ranch near us in Colorado, was talking with me one day about the Galapagos Islands. I mentioned my interest in islands in Maine. When I happened to speak of Swans Island, he suddenly showed great interest, and I soon realized it was Swan Island in the Caribbean which concerned him. He had been trying for many months to find the legal owner. I told him that it was owned by my good friend Sumner Smith and his family, and he said that if I would get an oil lease on it he would, "carry me for a one-half interest in an exploratory well." At that stage, he wouldn't tell me why he wanted it. I easily got the lease, and he told me that he understood there was an oil seep on the island and he wanted to fly down there and investigate it. At his invitation I went along. We flew to Grand Cayman in his big Convair and spent the night, transferring next morning to his Grumman Amphibian which flew us the 200 miles to Swan. At that time, condemned buildings belonging to several different departments of the U.S. government occupied most of its western shore. Although the island is about a mile long with some 500 acres, there seemed to be no calm water on which to land. When we touched down on top of a wave, I felt sure we would sink. We didn't and actually taxied to the beach and got ashore without getting wet above the knees. The reported oil seep consisted only of some black scum on the water from a shallow dug well. We took samples, but when we prepared to leave we found that the surge on the beach had driven our plane hard aground. It took the help of all the personnel left on the island to float and turn the plane around. We clambered aboard wet to the armpits. It took four attempts before we got airborne, in each of which we got bounced so badly that I was amazed the plane didn't disintegrate.

Tests on the samples of the black scum indicated that it was an asphalt base petroleum, but geologists were quite pessimistic that drilling would discover commercial production deeper in the limestone. We never did drill and ultimately gave up the lease after paying rentals for a number of years. Since then, the sovereignty of Swan Island has been given to Honduras by the United States.

Discussion with the Fish and Wildlife Service about the rookeries on Old Man and other islands has led to discussions of possibilities for conservation of other wild lands. Most important of these was my recommendation to Jim Barker that this agency would be suitable to act as owner and custodian of the large game preserve of which he was half owner, and which comprises the whole of Pinckney Island in South Carolina. I also suggested the same agency as custodian for the lands of Lawrence K. Marshall, comprising North Pack Monadnock Mountain in New Hampshire. Later I was instrumental in interesting another division of the Department of the Interior in acquiring some swamps and woods not far from the base of that mountain.

Another success in the field of conservation, which cost me nothing, involved Longfellow's Wayside Inn. Before World War II, we enjoyed riding with the Millwood Hunt over the fields of the inn which Mr. Henry Ford had bought. He was always very cordial to us and we admired the way he had furnished it as a museum with lovely colonial antiques, and the way he had adorned the grounds with an old grist mill, meeting-house, and school. When Mr. Ford died, his son had predeceased him, and his college-age grandsons were too young to take an interest. We heard the executors felt obliged to sell the property and were negotiating with a buyer who intented to convert it to a cheap ice cream parlor. Dr. Burt Wolbach asked me to contribute $10,000 toward a fund to save the property. He had collected $30,000 from others. I didn't turn him down, but suggested a better plan. I didn't think he would succeed because the competition would simply outbid him. Instead I went to Dean Donald David of the Harvard Business School. I knew that David had helped the executors find Ernest Breech to run Ford Motor Company. David agreed that a great many friends of Ford would be shocked at such a perversion of a priceless heritage and concurred with me that this would do far more damage to the good name of Ford and of his company than could be cured by many times as much money spent on advertising. He immediately got in touch with the executors who decided to convey the property to a non-profit

CHAPTER XVI

⤌⧫⤍

Travels

OUR love for Maine's islands spread to an interest in islands all over the globe. In the course of our travels we have visited many of the world's islands but not with a view to ownership. The larger ones we usually explored by automobile. Where there were roads, it was nearly always possible to hire a driverless car. We have driven thousands of happy miles on islands that a generation ago had no roads at all. Most of these we reached by air, and we especially enjoyed such less well known islands as Tierra del Fuego, Iceland, Greenland, Newfoundland, the Hebrides, Tahiti, Moorea, Bora Bora, Viti Levu, New Zealand, Madeira, the Azores, the Canaries, the Balearics, the Ionians, the Cyclades, the Dodecanese, Rhodes, Crete, Sicily, Malta, Gozo, Sardinia, and Corsica, as well as all the principal islands of the Greater and Lesser Antilles, some of the East Indies, the Galapagos, and several Alaskan islands.

Nowadays, most of our travel is for fun. We continue to make occasional visits to Central and South America, and more often to Europe. In the last few years we've done some horseback riding in Hungary and in Jamaica, some sightseeing in Yugoslavia and Greece, some bird watching on tributaries of the Amazon, and we've made two trips to Patagonia. On the most recent of these, we wanted to hire a driverless car in Buenos Aires and motor to the Straits of Magellan, then cross to Tierra del Fuego and camp whenever necessary en route. Our grandchildren recommended the newest in camping equipment, and we bought a complete outfit, including tent, sleeping bags, foam mattresses, cook stove, and dried food, all of which weighed only forty-five pounds and could be easily carried on a packframe. In Buenos Aires the company gave a cocktail party for us, and the guests made many recommendations that we must stay with their friends and relatives. In consequence, we never camped out a single night but stayed at various estancias, ending up at the Harberton Ranch on the Beagle Channel in southern Tierra del Fuego. We didn't motor all the way, but traveled by air the least interesting stretches. The camping equipment was left at Harberton as partial compensation for our delightful stay with the Goodall family. Most of the way we followed the Andes, crossing and recrossing the Continental Divide. This route provides magnificent views of many mountain lakes, including such large lakes as Nahual Huapi, Buenos Aires, Viedma, and Argentino. Although the Southern Andes are not very high, they are heavily glaciated and contain some of the most awesome spires in the world. The snowfield west of Lake Argentino is said to be the largest anywhere in the temperate zones. It feeds several glaciers, which bring great icebergs into the lake. Most notable is the Moreno Glacier, which has cut completely across Lake Argentino, blocking off the flow and causing a difference in level of the two parts of the lake. Icebergs calve off both sides of the glacier, falling with a roar and creating great waves every few minutes.

Because of glaciers flowing into the sea, it is not possible to motor all the way south along the west shore of southern Patagonia. One must leave the mountains in order to get around to the east of the lakes which extend many miles into the plains. Crossing the outlets to these lakes are government ferries, so that one can motor all the way to Punta Arenas. Because of the high winds, some of the country is rather desolate with large areas covered by wind-rounded pebbles and only an occasional stunted bush.

At one point on this trip we drove 130 miles from the nearest town to a sheep ranch in the foothills, arriving just at dark. We spent three days there exploring the mountains afoot. Our host insisted that a herder accompany us, and always at noon he produced a large haunch of lamb which was roasted on an open fire. The property comprised several hundred thousand acres immediately east of Mounts Fitzhugh and Torre. A large party of Spanish Alpinists with a huge amount of the latest Alpine equipment were camped just below the snow line. They were from Madrid and were financed by the state television company. They wanted to make a first ascent of Torre, but on their arrival they learned that an Italian party headed by Cesare Maestri had made the ascent ahead of them during an unprecedented twenty-two days of fair weather, using a gasoline-powered air compressor and air-powered drill to install iron pegs all the way up some 2,000 feet of the vertical rock face. The Spaniards' bivouac at the foot of the spire had been covered with more than a meter of snow while they were away climbing. The storm had buried some $10,000 worth of equipment, and they were unable to find it despite some two weeks of digging.

We also ran into a group of Australian climbers further south in the Andes among the Paine peaks and they, too, had some unkind remarks about the weather. The high winds, violent storms, and frequent clouds among the peaks add greatly to the difficulties of climbing in that part of the world.

Another interesting trip we made in recent years started as a business trip to establish a carbon black plant in the Union of South Africa. We motored through Krueger National Park down to Lourenço Marques in Moçambique and then through Swaziland and Natal to Durban and along the south coast following the Garden Route. We made visits to Basutoland, Griqualand, and the Transkei.

After several days in Capetown, with visits to Table Mountain, the Cape of Good Hope, and some of the lovely vineyard and orchard country of that southwest tip of Africa, we proceeded

northward through desert country and via Bloemfontain and Pre-
toria to the stupendous Victoria Falls, which dwarf Niagara. There
we crossed the Zambesi River and motored on through Rhodesia
to the Congo. It was just before the revolution in the Congo had
erupted, and I am using in this account the names of that period
in 1960 rather than the modern nomenclature. We visited the
cities of Bulawayo and Salisbury, and made a visit to the grave
of Cecil Rhodes in Matabeleland. We ferried the length of Lake
Tanganyika, drove from Usumbura to Bukavu where the Belgian governor of the province of Kivu, Mr. Willaert, gave a
luncheon party for us. Seated next to our host, I got into a discussion of the economics of his constituency using my schoolboy
French. I thought he was telling me of natural gas discovered
in Lake Kivu, and I pictured drilling rigs somewhere in the lake,
but when he mentioned a figure of 300 billion cubic meters, I
tried to tell him I thought he had the decimal in the wrong place.
This irritated him enough to call in a bilingual aide who confirmed
that he was talking about nine trillion cubic feet of gas, twenty-five
percent methane, not in the rock under the lake but in the water of
the lake itself. I was a bit incredulous. Three days later, after we
had visited Ruanda and Urundi, two Belgian engineers called on
us at our hotel in Goma. They took us to the site where an attempt was being made to exploit this enormous reserve of flam-
mable gas. There was a raft out a few hundred feet in the lake
with a plastic pipe suspended some 1,500 feet into the water.
From this a cloud of water vapor and gas was gushing. It was
easily ignited by an electric spark, but the flame tended to blow
out in a breeze.

On my return, I wrote about the hypothesis as to the origin
of this gas, and I believe that it was the first account written in
English, although a couple of papers in French had been published
in Belgium. At the time, the unique phenomenon was not known in
America by any of the many geologists with whom I was acquainted. Unfortunately, the political uncertainties of Kivu and lack of

Virginia and Linda inspect our newly purchased Butter Island in East Penobscot Bay, Maine, summer of 1942.

An osprey leaves his nest on one of our islands in Maine.

Avelinda anchored at Brimstone, an outer island of the Maine Coast.

Decorated by friends on seventieth birthday.

Executive Committee of the Board of Overseers crossing the Harvard Yard. Left to right: T. D. Cabot (Chairman of the Committee), F. Sargent Cheever, David Rockefeller (President of the Overseers), Douglas Dillon, John L. Loeb, Robert Hoguet, Robert Amory, Jr.

Four generations of Cabots. **Godfrey L. Cabot** on 100th birthday, February 21, 1961, with T.D.C., T.D.C., Jr., and **T.D.C., III.**

In 1970, Harvard voted me an honorary LL.D. to be awarded by
President Pusey at Commencement.

Dear Tom

Congratulations on your 80th birthday. I couldn't let the occasion pass without sending my very warmest greetings. I only hope you know how many friends and admirers you have in the University and how strongly they join with me in conveying our best wishes.

From my standpoint, it has been a great privilege and an even greater pleasure to have the opportunity to come to know you. You may not realize the effect you have on me and my colleagues. But in this difficult job, it is The greatest possible encouragement to know that there are persons like yourself who care about Harvard in the best way and for the best reasons. I count myself very fortunate to know you and look forward to continuing to work together for this wonderful institution that we have in common.

Warmest wishes, Derek

Chalet Rössli, our retreat and stable in Sharon, New Hampshire.

Carving a horse-trough and fountain for our chalet in Sharon, New Hampshire.

Our "retirement" chalet deep in the hills of southern New Hampshire.

capital in that part of the world have tended to retard development of this important resource. As far as I know, the gas is now used only in a minor way to supply the limited fuel needs of Goma.

I feel sure there is no other place in the world with a similar circumstance. The gas remains dissolved in a static 500-foot layer of salt water at the bottom of the lake in which organic matter falls from the 1,000-foot layer of fresh water above. Here it decays to form a gas similar to common marsh gas. Because of very high pressure and lack of convection currents, the gas remains dissolved. A pipe lowered to the gas-charged salt water acts much like a flowing oil well or "gusher."

From Goma we continued northward through King Albert Park to the Ituri Forest, where a Belgian friend introduced us to some of the pygmies. Later he gave us a chance to go hunting with these interesting people. What an amazing experience to silently walk through the jungle behind pygmies. They hear something move in the thick forest and stop and make weird calls to attract the game. Although sometimes they hunt with poisoned arrows, with us that day they were hunting with only spears. They got no large game, and they expressed great disappointment to us and assured us that the lack of success was not our fault.

We also visited the beautiful caves of Mount Hoyo that were used for the movie "King Solomon's Mines," and we stopped in the Ruwenzori Mountains. We were going to climb on Mount Stanley, but the weather took a threatening turn and we had to give up the expedition. We motored on to Murchison Falls in Uganda, where the enormous volume of the Nile flows out of Lake Victoria to plunge through a very narrow gorge dropping some 200 feet. A boat trip on the Nile below the falls gave us close-up views of elephants, hippos, crocodiles, and many other animals. Later we visited Queen Elizabeth Park and had several excitingly close encounters with herds of elephants and buffaloes. Then, continuing eastward, we visited the Ugandan cities of Kampala and Entebbe.

Following the African highlands from Capetown to the Upper Nile, one can see lots of beautiful country, but the animals are the most impressive. Let us hope that they can be preserved for the delight of posterity.

We flew from Entebbe to Nairobi and hired another driver-less car to motor south to Lake Amboseli Park. We continued to Arusha, where we stayed with the Pat Hemingways (son of the author). We also spent a night with a German family on the slopes of Mount Meru, where we saw some species of animals rarely found in national parks. We spent two days at Ngorongoro and two more in the Serengeti Plains. The crater of Ngorongoro surely has the highest concentration of wild game of any place in the world and is a photographer's paradise.

On our drive back to Arusha and Nairobi in our driverless car we had a serious breakdown, and it looked for a while as if we would be stranded with more than a day's walk to the nearest village. The forged yoke to one front wheel broke, leaving the wheel so awry that the fender rested on the tire. We managed to break off a hardwood branch from an acacia tree with which we propped up the car and tied the wheel support with wire strongly enough to limp back to Arusha where we could find a welding outfit.

From Nairobi we flew to Addis Ababa, Ethiopia, where we spent two days; then to Cairo, where we were pleasantly sur-prised at the amount of modernization that had taken place in the seventeen years since our previous visit.

The most interesting part of these African travels was the op-portunity to get a better understanding of their political problems. We had a good chance to see firsthand the effect of the apart-heid policy in South Africa, and to talk with critics of the Na-tional Party about the policies of black suppression. Undoubt-edly one of the main reasons we lost the chance to build a plant in that country was due to our disapproval of the government's racial policy. I came to realize how bitter were the differences between the two political parties of the so-called Caucasians. Africa was in turmoil at the time. The Belgian control of the Congo was crumbling and the Portuguese control of Moçambique was weakening. Independence for Basutoland and Swaziland was imminent. In East Africa, despite the terrorism of the Mau Maus, the government was still in white hands. Ethiopia under Haile Selassie still had a feudal aspect, but the better educated of the natives were obviously eager for change.

From a tourist standpoint, it was a notable trip despite our disappointment at losing the opportunity to build the first carbon black plant on that continent. We brought back pictures, both movies and stills, of scenery, animals, and natives which I have had the good fortune to talk about to numerous groups.

The short trips we have made to Africa since 1960 have reinforced our belief that we Americans must continue to support the principles of universal suffrage, majority rule, equal rights, and no racial discrimination. Unless we help when asked, the future looks bleak. Famines are inevitable and we must do more to control the growth in population.

CHAPTER XVII

❧

Higher Education

ALTHOUGH I never earned a post-graduate degree, higher education has been a matter of constant interest. My view on the deficiencies of education in our country have been fortified by my experiences abroad. The ignorance of our culture, revealed by Americans dealing in foreign countries, is often alarming. During my service in Washington, I accompanied an important presidential appointee on his first trip to Europe. He held a government position and earned degrees that would lead one to expect a familiarity with foreign cultures. We flew directly to Paris arriving the Saturday evening before Easter. There was no business to occupy us on Sunday and being warned that our hotel rooms were probably bugged, I thought it would serve both security and pleasure if we spent that Easter Day motoring to Chartres. Chatting as we drove, I was amazed to find he had never heard of feudalism or Gothic architecture and asked what I meant by peasant and Bourbon. He had almost no knowledge of the French Revolution and the Napoleonic Wars. When we arrived at our destination he was shocked to learn that Chartres and the other great cathedrals of Europe were Roman Catholic. It is hardly surprising that such ignorance in an American official should impair his ability to deal effectively with his counterparts in friendly governments abroad.

My two years in the hills of West Virginia also taught me the importance of education in the development of a community. Without good schools the rural counties stagnated. Resources were wasted and health impaired by ignorance and superstition.

And these deficiencies are not only among the rural poor. It is all too often that one finds a graduate of a good college who can't think quantitatively and shuns analytical thought. Perhaps this is because too much of our educational system is designed to help the student give correct answers to examination questions and not to think for themselves. Surely knowledge is less important than understanding. The creative thought needed for leadership cannot derive from facts alone. In seeking personnel for running our business, I have always looked for someone with basic logical thought. Perhaps it was this emphasis that has led to my close associations in the academic world.

I was elected a term member of the M.I.T. corporation in 1946 and a life member in 1951. I have also served on many visiting committees of that institution, often as chairman. It has been a great satisfaction to see the institute grow in my lifetime from a small, little-known technical school into the greatest technical university in the world.

Combining this experience with the experience as an overseer of Harvard has been especially satisfying. When first nominated for overseership I was defeated, but a second nomination in 1953 won me the necessary votes to qualify. Rarely is anyone nominated for a second term, but I had this privilege in 1962. I have been a member of the Harvard board for twelve years, and during these I was chairman of several of the board's more important committees.

The charter of Harvard gives its overseers a veto power which is rarely exercised. Visiting committees of the overseers are only advisory, but because the overseers represent the constituency that provides most of Harvard's large endowment, their advice is not taken lightly. This is not to say that the overseers tend to interfere with the faculty in academic matters, but in my experience, there were times when a visiting committee member, especially an overseer chairman, was very helpful in solving spe-

cific problems of an academic department. In my first term I had
two such problems. The first involved the future of the Meteo-
rological Observatory on Blue Hill. It was decided by the corporation to discontinue the observatory on the retirement of the
professor in charge. Lawyers rendered an opinion that the endowment income could be legally used in Cambridge. But it was
apparent that the families who contributed to this endowment
were going to be very unhappy, and with the help of the Astron-
omy Department and the Dean I was able to work out a plan
to bring to Harvard a brilliant atmospheric physicist from Cambridge, England. The support of his research with government
funds allowed the observatory to continue.

The other problem involved criticism of the offshoot of the
former Harvard engineering school. Graduates of that school,
especially those with a private practice as engineering consul-
tants, felt badly let down that Harvard had dropped the word
"engineering" from its curriculum. I spent a great deal of time
with members of the Harvard Engineering Society who were leading this attack and was able to persuade them that Harvard could
not find the funds to run an orthodox program in engineering
and that the value of a Harvard degree would be better protected
by improving the quality of research and teaching in areas of engineering and applied physics in which Harvard was already strong.
It took a great many letters and visits to other cities to persuade
the opposition, but I was able to make progress with help from
friends in other engineering schools.

Also while an overseer, I worked on various programs to develop financial support for Harvard. I am proud of my successes
in getting large grants from alumni not known for their generosity to Harvard.

One of these undertakings led to an amusing incident which
I tell about at money-raising meetings when called on to exhort
the solicitors. Virginia and I were visiting the Fiji Islands, in
the Melanesian area of the southwest Pacific, and were driving

across the island of Viti Levu from the Nandi airport to the city of Suva. It was a wearisome trip on a rough and dusty road. Virginia complained of a headache and I was tired from driving when we came to an attractive hotel on the shore. We stopped, and leaving her on a couch with a couple of aspirin tablets, I put on my trunks and went down to the beach. There was only one other bather there, a handsome brunette in a bikini with a voluptuous figure who was gamboling in the surf. I jumped over a few waves myself and presently said to her: "Do you speak English?"

"Certainly," she replied with an American accent.

"Where are you from?", I asked.

"Cleveland."

Having made this progress successfully, I held out my hand and said, "My name is Tom Cabot."

This brought the immediate response: "Oh, I know you, you're the biggest beggar in Boston."

That my fame had spread all the way to that remote archipelago tickled my vanity and I soon found out that she was married to a Cleveland industrialist and they were vacationing at the hotel, so I asked if they would dine with us. Over cocktails, I learned that he was a vice-president of Sohio and a close friend of an elderly Cleveland man who had graduated from Harvard before me and whose name had been given me to solicit in the Program for Harvard College. This was an $82.5 million dollar campaign that we successfully completed during my first term as an overseer of the college.

This well-known alumnus, chairman of a large publicly-owned company, had never given Harvard more than $1,000.

Following the rule book for successful solicitation, I had studied my prospect's biography and by reference to proxy statements and a report from Dunn & Bradstreet, I learned he had no children, a comfortable bank balance and no substantial debt and that he held $9 million worth of stock in his company.

Three times I tried unsuccessfully to make an appointment to come to Cleveland to see him. It became apparent that he was determined to avoid me. Not content with a telephone call or letter, I was determined on a face-to-face interview. I learned that he was coming to Boston to speak at a seminar in Endicott House which is in Dedham, about twenty miles from Logan Airport. It was very easy for my secretary to find out that he was coming in his company's executive plane, and for me to get the expected time of arrival from Butler Aviation, which services private planes at Logan. So I was there to meet him and offer a ride, which he could hardly refuse, this being a part of the airport where there are not taxis waiting.

Now I had a captive audience, and the rest was easy. He gave $100,000. I am sure his happiness in life has been enhanced. In fact, he told me that he had grown up a poor boy and hadn't yet learned the pleasure of being generous; that he still darned his own socks and hated to tip. But, as we parted he said he felt better from having promised me the hundred thousand for Harvard. And, on returning to Cleveland he told his friends about how he had been "worked over by a real pro."

My efforts to raise money were not always so successful. I tried to raise funds for a new laboratory for Harvard's chemistry department in the early 1960's. Harvard was then turning down a very large proportion of applicants for graduate studies in chemistry, especially postdoctoral fellows. Even when they applied with adequate financial support, Harvard lacked the laboratory space. Although I couldn't find the money at that time, President Pusey and the corporation decided to have a general solicitation known as the Program for Science. Included in this program were the funds for a laboratory for chemistry and biology to be located on Divinity Avenue. Largely from a charitable trust established by my father, I was able to pledge a substantial sum, but the total support for the program was disappointing and the proposal for the laboratory was abandoned. The $4.5 million dollars which I had raised for it was used to name for my father the library of the new general science building on Kirkland Street, and to establish a science professorship in my name.

In addition to being an overseer of Harvard, I still serve as a trustee of Radcliffe. I have long advocated a greater enrollment of women in Harvard University, and it is now a great satisfaction to see how the opportunity for women in higher education has improved over the years. In the early years of Radcliffe, Harvard professors were hired to teach the young women at Radcliffe in their spare time. During the manpower shortage of World War II a new arrangement was made under which most of the teaching was in mixed classes and degrees for both sexes became a responsibility of Harvard. After the war, the responsibility of the Radcliffe board was largely confined to the admission, housing, feeding, and chaperoning of women studying at Harvard. Now most of these responsibilities have gradually been taken over by Harvard giving women full access to all Harvard has to offer.

An important change which caused much debate was the question of co-residence. Because I was reared by Victorian parents, I first thought this quite unacceptable, but frank discussions with students and masters have made a convert of me. There is now good evidence that the arrangement is far better for intellectual and social development and my inquiries would indicate that morality in the truest sense has not declined. The students of today have a code that can be followed to good purpose, with good conscience, and without hypocrisy.

In addition to serving the institutions of higher education in the Boston area, I have interested myself in smaller institutions serving minority and underprivileged groups. While with United Fruit Company, I joined in establishing an agricultural school in Zamorano, Honduras, for Spanish-speaking natives of Central America. Originally its students enrolled with only a grammar school education, but today most of its students have a high school diploma. Emphasis is on field work to a far greater ex-

tent than in agricultural colleges in the United States. Because
students work longer hours with shorter vacations they cover
nearly as much ground in three years as other schools cover in
four. Graduates show a good record and are in great demand
throughout the American tropics.

I have also been a trustee of Hampton Institute in Virginia,
have chaired the Board of Visitors of the Fletcher School at Tufts,
and have served in an advisory capacity on schools dealing with
students from the emerging countries of Africa and Asia and have
occasionally been given the opportunity to lecture on problems
of trade and investment in these developing parts of the world.

Cynics say that universities raise money by degrees and possibly some of my honorary degrees were bestowed more for my
pocketbook than for my wisdom. My doctorate from Harvard can,
I think, be attributed to my loyalty, for I have cherished that
great university from early childhood. We are a Harvard family.
My father, my grandfather, most of my uncles, my two brothers,
and all of my children went to Harvard. I wish more of my grandchildren had also had that experience.

I am glad that I have been able to establish a University Professorship in Science at Harvard and an Institute Professorship
at M.I.T. That these bear my name is of little importance at the
moment, but the two incumbents are very distinguished scientists and if others as bright follow them, perhaps the chairs will
really be a meaningful honor after a few generations. As an illus-
tration of how unimportant the name is at the moment I should
say that the first two incumbents were next door neighbors in
Lexington and neither knew that the other was a Thomas Dudley Cabot Professor until I introduced the subject. One is Ma-
thew Meselson, who had a part in resolving the secrets of DNA,
and the other is Sam Ting, who was a co-discoverer of the
J-particle.

The money I have found for the educational institutions of
Greater Boston would have been much greater if a venture in

television had succeeded. Ted Jones, a very well-meaning neighbor of mine in Weston who has since become a Unitarian minister, came to me in December 1962 to suggest that I join him in applying to the Federal Communications Commission for Channel 5, then assigned to the *Boston Herald*. He thought that with his management and $100,000 of my money we would have a thirty percent chance of winning a license worth at least $20 million. His dollar estimates, we found in the end, were too low by a factor of more than three, and it took not a few weeks, but about ten years of work and worry, all to no avail, for we lost.

We undertook the effort not for profit, but for charity. The company we formed was to be owned by a charitable foundation, all the earnings being dedicated to schools, colleges, museums, and the arts in the area served by the television channel. We recruited a dozen other well-known philanthropists to join us in the project. The hearings in Washington took many months and filled many large volumes with testimony, pleadings, and exhibits. I think the record of the case weighed more than half a ton. The legal bills of all the contestants probably totaled at least $2,500,000. And I don't think any one of us, winner or loser, could give a good answer as to how or why the commission decided as it did. Quinlan's *The Hundred Million Dollar Lunch* is a dramatic book about the case and tells how the *Herald* lost, but offers no clear clue as to how the winner won.

We had good lawyers and made a good presentation and I prefer to think that the commission felt that we might have been the ablest of the contestants in 1962, but were too old to start a new business when they finally came to their decision nearly ten years later.

CHAPTER XVIII

⟨✦⟩

Philanthropy

DESPITE my retirement from business, I still prefer going to the office regularly. Broadly defined my major activity is philanthropy, but this covers a wide field. Occasionally I raise money for a good cause if convinced it deserves a very high priority in any giving program. More often, I study proposals to our own foundation trying to decide which are worthy of support. In many respects the decisions are more difficult than those one meets running a business. It is rare to find any quantitative measure of what to expect a grant will do for human welfare. And studies of the effects of earlier grants usually leave one in a quandary as to which were really successful.

Believing that a great deal of philanthropic money was wasted in the community, our foundation took the lead in forming the Associated Foundations of Greater Boston to study inner city problems on a cooperative basis. Arthur Phillips, our director, was its first president. My own specialty has been hospitals and health care and how to control cost without impairing quality.

In May of 1968, Dean Ebert of Harvard Medical School asked me to head a committee to raise $15 million for the Affiliated Hospitals Center of which Stan Deland was president. They proposed a new building in the Longwood area to house the hospital activities carried out at four other locations. I tried to beg off on the ground that I was seventy-one at that time. He explained that he had chosen me for this job because he couldn't pick a leader from any of the hospitals involved without creating jealousy, and because of my knowledge of Harvard, of hospitals and of Boston philanthropists. I agreed to take the job, thinking it would take six months. It took more than six years. I built up what I thought was a good team for solicitation and approached hospital trustees and other large prospects in preparation for the start of the formal campaign in March of 1969. In early April, some radical students occupied University Hall in Cambridge, demanding that Harvard stop evicting tenants from properties needed for expansion. During the previous twenty years Harvard had bought the old frame buildings on the site selected, promising to make it available for the hospital when needed. It soon became apparent that, although all leases had expired, it would be impossible to oust tenants without eviction proceedings, and these Harvard was not prepared to undertake. Many months were spent studying alternatives, and in the meantime the whole campaign ground to a halt. We couldn't ask for gifts to build a hospital for which we had no site. Costs were escalating and political opposition to the project was growing. The campaign for an acceptable site and a means of financing construction dragged on for years. We have now raised more money than the original goal, but the final plan is more than twice as costly as originally expected. We have merged the four original hospitals into one corporate ownership and have cleared a site which has met community acceptance. Funds have been borrowed and construction started. We feel confident that the new building will add immensely to keeping Harvard and Boston preeminent in the field of health care.

My association in this joint venture, as well as my much longer association with other hospitals, especially The Children's Hospital and Massachusetts General Hospital, have done much to stimulate my interest in the whole subject of health care. I have written several articles on the subject of cost and how to control it. These have stimulated ongoing correspondence with doctors and economists here and abroad.

It is my view that the fee-for-service system traditional among medical practitioners is a piecework system without the normal controls. The consumer has little or no chance to decide what tests, therapies, and hospitalization to buy. The decision is made by the provider. Few could afford to let any other type of provider decide the quality and quantity of his purchases. And in the practice of medicine there is added to the profit motive to overprovide, the additional motive of malpractice complaints should the provider fail to make any relevant test, or prescribe an indicated therapy or operation. Substituting a system where the consumer pays regularly to be kept well, rather than for service when he is sick, gives the practitioner an incentive more sensitive to the ratio of benefit to cost. Such a system is not just a fee paid monthly by the consumer to an insurer such as Blue Cross, but a health maintenance organization (HMO) in which the providers are hired to keep one well and have the incentive to get one well as quickly and cheaply as possible should sickness come. Nor is it a scheme to pay for all health care from the public purse. HMO's are operating successfully in many communities at considerable saving in cost and with satisfactory results. The HMO established by Harvard to serve Greater Boston is my especial interest. Here it was not possible to establish in an old community a closed panel system eliminating fee-for-service at all levels of health care, but with the primary care providers paid a basic salary, plus a bonus for reductions in the capitation fee, there is incentive to monitor the charges of specialists and hospitals to avoid not only overcharges but more especially the charges for unnecessary tests, therapies, and hospitalization.

The cost of the adversary process of determining malpractice contributes enormously to the bill for health costs in this country. It is not only the high insurance premiums but also the defensive medical practices which must be collected from all patients. The incompetent or negligent doctor is protected by insurance from payment for his faults. Few claimants get anything and those that do are rewarded too late to help with their need and in amounts that are largely based on pain and suffering rather than economic loss. The occasional large awards are apt to remove the recipient from productive work and certainly can't obliterate pain or restore happiness. Indeed, it is a bad system on almost every count.

New Zealand and Australia have adopted a better system. Although tort litigation never approached as high a level of cost there as here, they concluded that the adversary process was too capricious, wasteful, and ineffective. They have substituted for it the concept that all injuries as a result of accident are a community responsibility and that every victim should receive his net economic loss. Instead of the nearly impossible task of fixing blame, which does little to reduce accidents and injuries, they are now relying on strict licensure to reduce negligence and incompetence.

For some years, I have tried to convince legislators to adopt similar legislation here. There has been some progress in Massachusetts that tightens up the licensing of doctors and imposes a preliminary screening of malpractice claims before they are tried in court. This may slow the rise in rates of insurance, but it does not eliminate the wasteful efforts of trying to determine blame.

My interest in this came about during my directorship in American Mutual Liability Insurance Company. I found we were losing money on malpractice insurance and tried to get the management to abandon the business, which they eventually did. My interest, however, rapidly expanded from the question of profit and loss to the far broader problem of engineering a system that would be more beneficial to society as a whole. I prefer the term "social engineering" for such studies, and this has been my approach. An engineer thinks in terms of mechanical advantage or levers by which a small initial force can overcome large resistance. An industrialist thinks in terms of incentives by which he can get maximum productivity from his co-workers. I try to devise plans for approaching social problems by similar means.

A few years ago, the rapid rise in cost of malpractice insurance prompted a study which revealed that for Harvard and its teaching hospitals the malpractice insurance premiums were some fifty times the actual payments to claimants. Tom Pyle of Harvard Community Health Plan asked my help in setting up a captive insurance company to cover this preferred risk. Having failed to get the Massachusetts legislature to eliminate the adversary process of determining malpractice, I joined forces with him to convince the many administrators, trustees, and practitioners of these Harvard affiliates that his plan had merit. After several months of intensive study, we established Controlled Risk Insurance Company (CRICO), domiciled in Grand Cayman Island. In its first year, this company saved the Harvard group three million dollars in premiums and also accumulated another three million dollars in unallocated reserves. The future looks promising, but of course it is impossible to predict the true savings.

I am proud that I turned over to my son Louis most of my business responsibilities when I was only sixty-three. Now that I am more than eighty and look back at my successes and failures, I feel more than ever the importance of decisiveness. When faced with a decision, I was rarely sure of the right path, nor can I say today with surety which decisions were right, but I am sure that indecision would have led only to failure.

Now I fear that indecisiveness is one of the greatest threats to the future of our country. The founders of our Constitution gave great power to the executive branch of our government, but to guard us against tyranny made it responsive to the ballot box, subject to law, and separate from the legislative and judiciary functions. In recent years we have created a fourth branch of government, the independent agencies, which are subject to law but not responsive to the ballot box. In theory they are responsible to Congress, but Congress can exercise control only by repealing the laws under which they were created. They are indeed independent and exercise powers which are both executive and judicial and are of enormous economic importance. I refer especially to FPC, FCC, FTC, ICC, CAB, and SEC, but there are many more. It is difficult to discover the policies which guide them, or the criteria on which their decisions are based. In fact, their decisions are often inconsistent with previous orders and could perhaps be called capricious. In consequence, when a needed project is presented, the hearings can last many months and cover thousands of pages with testimony and exhibits. No commissioner could possibly find time to read more than a small fraction of this. Naturally, most of the hearing record has no relevance to the decision. The cost of these hearings must all be added to what the consumer pays. The total cost, including the cost of delays, must add scores of billions of dollars to our cost of living.

My opinion of some of these agencies is prejudiced by personal experiences. I can't see why we need to allocate the radio and television licenses to those whose interest is in commercial advertising, but if we must, the profits should be returned largely to government by auctioning the channels as we do with oil leases on government land. And I don't see why we need to regulate the price of gas or oil at the point of production where there are thousands of producers competing. The economics of drilling for oil and gas is not so very different from farming. Both have become capital intensive industries with widely dispersed ownership and are keenly competitive.

For more than ten years, FPC has had ample opportunity to decide whether to ban or encourage the import of liquid natural gas. It still has not reached a decision, except the decision that it had no jurisdiction, and this it reversed after $130 million had been invested. Recently on a visit to Norway I saw five huge LNG tankers moored together at Kopervik, none of which had ever been used. It must be costing several hundred thousand dollars per day for them to be idle awaiting an FPC decision. How can investors now be expected to provide the capital needed to solve our energy crisis when faced with such uncertainty?

Europe and Canada are ready and eager to buy LNG. Overseas gas producers can get to market almost immediately in those countries, whereas to reach our markets here they must give options which delay for years all hope of income from sales.

As a result of the FPC indecision, which already has kept the Staten Island LNG facility idle for more than four years during a critical gas shortage in the New York–New Jersey area, the largest supplier to that area is proposing to build a duplicate facility at St. John, New Brunswick, which the Canadians would welcome. Already rights-of-way are being sought to pipe the gas back to New York. This will add several billion dollars to the cost of the gas to consumers in the New York area.

Throughout my career I have argued against monopolies and in favor of freer trade. To me it seems clear that free competition is the best assurance that providers will sell their goods and services at the least cost. Of course there are situations where competition is not feasible and regulation becomes necessary. We could hardly permit competing gas, water, or telephone companies to tear up the street to construct duplicate mains. But for the most part, the regulation by these independent agencies is unnecessarily adding to the cost of living by preserving monopolies where competition would benefit consumers.

Our society is far more complex and interdependent than it was when our government structure was adopted. This makes a clear division between its functions the more important. Independent regulatory agencies have done more to protect than to control concentrations of power. I would return freedom of choice to the consumers. It is our freedoms which have won the admiration of people everywhere, and the freedom of the consumer to choose how he will spend his money is no less sacred than other freedoms guaranteed to us by our Constitution.

I have written elsewhere of my brief service in the executive branch of government. I am glad I went to Washington for a year. The experiences added to my understanding and enjoyment of the problems we face as a nation. I came to have a warm regard for many of the career personnel in our government. Only indirectly were the experiences helpful in my business career. The skills needed in Washington were usually different from those required in a competitive business, but the elements of leadership and of human relations were no different. Decisions are more complex when dealing with foreign policy, but decisiveness is equally essential.

Experience and wisdom are not the same. I try to remember this when giving advice. I am not apt to be asked for advice as to life style nor could I cause much to change if I were asked. I respect the admonitions of my parents to put duty ahead of pleasure. I am sure the youngsters who scoff at ambition are missing lots of fun, and as they grow older, will miss the extreme satisfaction of an ambition fulfilled. Scoff if they wish at the Puritan virtues piety, sobriety, chastity, frugality, and diligence, but a life without dedication can never be a happy one.

As so I close with the thoughts so ably expressed by Samuel Gilman in the final lines of Harvard's hymn:

> Let not mosscover'd error moor thee at its side,
> As the world on truth's current glides by,
> Be the herald of light, and the bearer of love,
> Till the stock of the Puritans die.

APPENDIX

Avelinda *Wins the Lambert Cup Race*
New London to Marblehead—June 1938

When this good ship was nearly new
And I was young and active too
I put her in an ocean race
To see how well she'd stand the pace.

The race I picked was thought the best
To give my yacht a thorough test.
It came in June when I had planned
To see how Harvard fared on land
Against the Eli hordes at games,
And on the waters of the Thames
At matching strokes with Yale's best crew
Since first the sons of Yale wore blue.

Of course you know how Harvard did;
And how we rode a stormy tide
Around the Cape to Marblehead
In record time, you've probably read;
But now I want to tell you how
We carried sail through all that blow,
And how we won the silver cup
That Gerald Lambert had put up.

(Ballad as written by Winsor Gale):

The summary tells how the race came out
But I'd like to add how it came about
And a few other points about the race,

The papers missed through lack of space.
The time may come when you'll want to remember
What happened that week on the *Avelinda*.

I am generally known as a cruising man
And that is the way this trip began,
But as I thought, I began to see
That the race *from* New London appealed to me.

Of course, I like to see Harvard row,
But I wondered, too, if my boat could go.
So I carefully picked from the men I knew
Just the ones for a balanced crew.
First Ned Billings, steady and willing,
With plenty of weight for heavy pulling,
Whose deep-sea poise you couldn't rattle
And would be at his best in the heat of battle.
Then Win Gale, whose racing knowledge
Goes from kindergarten up to college.
Elliot Hedge was one I wanted
And Bob Livermore, whom nothing daunted.
These two, along with Alan Beede,
Supplied the endurance I felt I needed.
Then Bruce Edmands, the permanent fixture,
Did double duty as a curious mixture.
He could do the cooking like a regular cook
And on the light sails, he had what it took.
Pride filled my heart as I took along, too,
Thomas, the Junior, to round out the crew.

The equipment I needed took lots of thought,
When you're racing, and need it, it can't be bought.
The compass developed a curious bubble,
So I sent for a new one to eliminate trouble.
The charts and cable and log were checked,
And lots of things you'd never suspect.

Only one thing seemed lacking, it was nearly a slip,
I needed a sail that would *move* the ship.
So I ordered a spinnaker, biggest they made,
Twice as wide as the pole and that reached to the head.
With everything loaded and carefully stored,
We were ready to sail and tumbled aboard.

Pushing out from Cohasset on Tuesday night,
We ran down to Duxbury while it was light;
On through the canal on Wednesday morning,
The wind being light, the motor was running.
South Dartmouth was reached along about four
And our crew increased when we picked up two more,
Win Gale and Hedge, coming on together,
Hot, tired and thirsty and blaming the weather.
Bright and early next morning, a boat from the shore
Brought along Ned and Bob Livermore.
To run to New London took the rest of the day,
And close to Burr's Landing was the place where we lay.

Early next morning, with the sky bright and clear,
We pushed up the river for the race of the year.
With Harvard unbeaten and Yale the same way,
The best crews in the country were rowing that day.
The two morning races were coming down stream.
So we picked out a berth with the finish abeam.
The Freshmen, rowed first, was Harvard a length
And so was the Jay-Vee, smooth rowing plus strength.

With this pleasant beginning, we relaxed a few moments
And chatted a while with our next day's opponents.
The *Pole Star* lay close, she was sturdy though small.
Next to her was *Tioga*, seventy-three over all.
Along up the river was Greenough's *White Lady*
With a star afterguard, she was patently ready.

So on through the fleet we wended our way
To the three-mile mark for the race of the day.
When picking up Tommy, who had come down by train,
We found him and lost him and found him again.

With joking and laughter the afternoon passed,
Till the radio shouted "They've started" at last.
High in the crosstrees we gazed down the river,
Trying to pick out the Crimson-oared sliver.
And then when they finally came into sight,
We could see that Old Harvard was leading a might.
With Chace stroking smoothly a cool thirty-two,
And Yale one beat higher, he was holding the Blue,
Then raising the stroke, as Yale still hung on,
He met Yale's last spurt and Harvard had won.

Now for most of the crowd, this ended the fuss,
But it just marked the start of the racing for us.
So we anchored down river at the mouth of the bay
To be near the start of the racing next day.
While most of my crew went ashore for some fun,
I worked on board ship on last things to be done.
When I took off my clothes and crawled into bed,
We were set for the race to Marblehead.

The start was set for half-past nine.
We motored out to the starting line.
I cast my eye on the entry sheet
And knew *White Lady* the boat to beat.
The sea was flat as the old mill pond
Without a breath of air beyond.
If when wind came it was dead ahead,
Then all would beat us to Marblehead,
But if by chance it was from the west,
We would have the chance we liked the best.

Appendix

We drifted around till long about ten.
The wind we had missed started blowing again.
A glance at the compass and Heaven be blessed,
The first gentle cat's paw was from the southwest.
The starting gun boomed and sent us away
On our trek 'round Cape Cod and across the Bay.

The first leg of course was around Fisher's Island
With a favoring current as we came close to land.
Though the wind was quite fluky, we hung close together.
Here *White Lady* went past us, close on our weather.
But she went a bit far beyond the first buoy
And we slipped by inside her and laughed at her crew.
It was here that I taught my crew their first lesson
By keeping on out as the wind started to freshen,
For further on out, it blew more and more,
While all the large boats were becalmed in towards shore.

When set, the ballooner was doing right well
And bowled us along toward Block Island's bell.
At this point in the race I had only in mind
One thought and that was, keep *White Lady* behind.
Now with the wind blowing seventeen knots,
The *Huntress*, *Tioga* and other large yachts
Started feeling their length and going on by us
As if trying to say "You cannot deny us."
And frankly, the *Gypsy* looked good to us, too,
As she led all the rest and passed from our view.
The boats we were racing were boats of our size,
So the price for Class B was what dazzled our eyes.

Coming into Vineyard Sound
And up along the Middle Ground,
We hardly dared to look around,
For, like a greyhound newly freed,

The great *White Lady* showed her speed
And length by length cut down our lead.

The wind had freshened, bit by bit,
Till off West Chop it really hit
A blow that has some heft in it
And then what racing men all fear,
The light ballooner showed a tear,
So off it came for a quick repair.

Until six o'clock, when the watch was changed
The race, for us, had been well arranged.
The wind was fresh and looked here to stay
And the tide, for the most part, was going our way.

But now as we headed for Handkerchief Shoals,
'Twas a different hand that held the controls.
The wind was now blowing against the tide,
Building up waves like a mountain side.
Two helmsmen were needed to hold the ship off
To keep her from broaching as she dropped in the trough.
And here the *White Lady* finally caught us
As she slid through the tumult that nightfall had brought us.
The light at her masthead shone like a star
As we followed her through over Monomoy's Bar.
Once through The Slew, we turned up the shore,
Thankful to be in deep water once more.

But *White Lady* was out there, somewhere in the night.
And we knew that to hold her, we needed the kite.
Though the wind that was blowing had us down to the rail,
The sea was much smoother, so we hoisted the sail.
And now with great blasts coming off of the land,
Avelinda gave proof what a good boat can stand.
As each puff would strike her down, she would heel
With two, and yes three, strong men at the wheel.

But now we were gaining on Greenough at last
And would catch him again if we kept in our mast.
Then out from the shore came one mighty puff
That convinced us we'd carried the jib long enough.
With all hands on deck, it was doused on the run
Down just in time, but its job had been done,
For we caught the *White Lady* and passed her again
As they luffed up the roll a reef in her main.

The finish was forty miles away.
We headed out across the Bay.
Cape Cod had given some protection
From squalls that blew in that direction.
The ship now felt the wind's full power
When blowing forty miles per hour.
This was the peak, she stood the test,
And proved to be one Alden's best.

Though bowling along with a comfortable lead,
We searched for ideas for increasing our speed,
For in back of our minds from the very beginning
Lay the Lambert Cup and our chances of winning.
Of course, the *Huntress* was far out ahead,
Could she lead us four hours to Marblehead?
So we set the jib-topsail and added a knot
To the speed of our already fast-moving yacht.
And before this fair wind had a chance to diminish
With *White Lady* well beaten, we drove for the finish.

But it wasn't the *Huntress* we had to beat,
For *Tioga* had turned in a wonderful feat
And set a new record over the course
Of eighteen hours and yet she lost!
For *Avelinda*, with twenty-one plus
And four hours off, had won for us.

BEGGAR ON HORSEBACK

was printed in an edition of 4000 copies by The
Stinehour Press and The Meriden Gravure Company. The type, Monotype Bell, is a traditional face,
closely related to the French designs of Didot and
Fournier. It was first cut in 1788 by Richard Austin,
a professional engraver, and issued by John Bell of
London, a publisher, bookseller, typefounder, and
printer whose avowed ambition was 'to retrieve and
exalt the neglected art of printing in England.' The
type used in this edition was recut for the Monotype
Corporation of London in 1930 under the supervision
of Stanley Morison. The paper is Warren's Antique
66, an entirely groundwood- and acid-free sheet. The
book has been bound by Robert Burlen & Sons.
Calligraphy by Stephen Harvard.